GOD
day
by
day

Herbert F. Smith, S.J.

Our Sunday Visitor, Inc.
Huntington, Indiana 46750

The Nihil Obstat and Imprimatur are official declarations that a book or pamphlet is free of doctrinal or moral error. No implication is contained therein that those who have granted the Nihil Obstat or Imprimatur agree with the contents, opinions or statements expressed.

Imprimi Potest:
JACOB L. CONNOR, S.J.
Provincial, Maryland Province
Jesuit Fathers

Nihil Obstat:
REV. LAWRENCE GOLLNER
Censor Librorum

Imprimatur:
✠ LEO A. PURSLEY, D.D.
Bishop of Fort Wayne-South Bend

ISBN: 0-87973-866-9
Library of Congress Catalog Card Number: 73-84545

Cover Design by James E. McIlrath
Published, printed and bound in the U.S.A. by
Our Sunday Visitor, Inc., Huntington, Indiana 46750
866

FOREWORD

Everything human suffers with the passage of time. Time fudges everything over with irrelevancies, and it occasions the accumulation of the dead branches of obsolescence. Time allots the partisans opportunity to distort reality in the name of fidelity.

All of these forces of disease and decay affect religion. It is almost unbelievable how far religion can become diseased. When we look to the cause, however, we understand. Religion is a powerful force in men's lives. Unsullied, it stands in the path of all who lust for an excess of power. Corrupted, it augments the power of the powerful. So it comes about that all who have too much power, or seek too much, seek to corrupt religion by subjugating it.

It is a dangerous mistake to think that only those who are in search of raw power corrupt religion. To some, power is only a means to an ostensibly nobler goal. Many a militant idealist makes religion over into his image and likeness, to serve his purposes, which may be laudably humanistic, but are hardly religious. His use of religion is idolatrous, as is every employment of religion as a means instead of an end. God deliver us from the do-gooders, clerical or lay, who subvert the highest order of reality in making it a servant of their own goodness.

Religion so used becomes a catchall for do-goodism. It becomes a verbal hamper into which every more-or-less selfless human undertaking is thrown. Its reality is buried under the accumulation. God is extruded from religion. The passion is put out, and not much is asked or demanded any more, except in the name of someone's own pet project.

These reflections are an attempt to see religion for what it really is. Religion is man turned to God. In fact, the Christian religion does not begin with man at all, but with God. It is God's thoughts that are primary, not man's. It is God's plan that is important, not man's. It is the passion for God that is central, not the passion for mankind. It is what God can do for mankind that counts, not what a man thinks he can do for mankind by using religion as a lever to pry moral conduct out of his fellowmen. Even religious leaders not infrequently resort to these tactics of misusing religion. It becomes a vise to squeeze out of people an attitude of brotherhood, or a club to beat them into being pacifists. What folly! There is no such shortcut to the fruit of religion. If men cannot be led to the love of God, which will inspire them to do these things because of what they become, they will not be persuaded to do them at all.

The reflections that follow are an effort to hammer away the encrustations befouling religion. They cut away dead branches. They cry out against every perversion of religion, however popular. Perversion is man's doing and deserves no respect, but true religion is God's doing and forbids all hedging.

I offer these reflections on Scripture and today's society, not as a means to use religion for the advance of society, but as a means to subject society to God. That is true religion. The reward will be finding God day by day. The bonus will be the propelling of society into the brightest possible future. Society is blessed only when it is an expression of man's right relation with God. It may look at a glance as though religion is an element of society, but the truth is that society is an expression of religion — or irreligion. The shape of society is a measure of how we are faring in our relationship with God.

These pages attempt to stir up the fire of the passion for God through reflection on His word in the light of our times. They invite you to burn with a new zeal by seeing more clearly the place of God in our daily lives, and feeling more purely the electrifying hope which only pure and undefiled religion can awaken in mankind.

Herbert Francis Smith, S.J.

Table of Contents

PART ONE

1—A Father's Love 13
2—The Young Will Be Free 16
3—Family Life 20
4—The Marriage Parable 24
5—Youth Feel Betrayed 27
6—Companionship 30
7—A Pattern for Personhood 33
8—The Human Jesus 36
9—Conquest of Temptation 39
10—The Service of Life 43
11—Faith in Faith 46

PART TWO

12—The Battle of Faith 51
13—Suffering 55
14—Hope 59
15—Love 62
16—Gratitude 65
17—Joy 68
18—Self-Esteem 71
19—The Meaning of Mary 74

PART THREE

20—Revelation 79
21—Change in the Church 83
22—New Doctrines 86
23—Christian Witness 89
24—Ways to Encounter God 92
25—The Parable of Hope 96
26—Authority: Our Firmest Hope 100
27—Christianity Unfenced 103

PART FOUR

28—The Anawim 109
29—Our New Neighbors 113
30—Honesty 116
31—Lived Religion 120
32—Responsibility 124
33—God's Place in Religion 128
34—Who God Is 131
35—True Religion 135
36—Foundations of Religion 138

37—Trying to Love God 141
38—Man's Master 144
39—Venus or Christ? 147

PART FIVE

40—Freedom 153
41—Bad Faith 156
42—The Means to Discover Christ 159
43—The Transmission of Life 163
44—Religion Gives Life 166
45—God's Relevance to Man 169
46—Transformation of Man 172
47—God's Devotion 176
48—Architect of the Future 179
49—Suffering Preludes Theophany 182
50—We Have a King 185
51—Cosmic Continuity 188

PART ONE

1

A Father's Love

If God is our Father, why are we struggling as though alone? Why do we go down in defeat after defeat? Why did the Apostle Paul suffer so much he had to warn his people against despairing at the spectacle: "Brethren, I beg you not to be disheartened by the trials I endure for you"?

"I kneel before the Father. . . ." Paul goes on. Why did the heavenly Father Paul so revered permit Paul's sufferings? Is a father's love cold? Or harsh? What then? What is the nature of a father's love?

The tender, sweet, consoling quality of a true mother's love is known to all of us, and God draws on this knowledge to invite us to an understanding of His own fatherly love for us: "Does a woman forget her baby at the breast, or fail to cherish the son of her womb? Yet even if these forget, I will not forget you."

Through Jeremiah, however, we also hear this: "The Lord said to me: 'Do not pray for the welfare of this people. Though they fast I will not hear their cry and though they offer burnt offerings and cereal offerings I will not accept them; but I will consume them by the sword, by famine, and by pestilence!' "

Here then is the difficulty. We recognize the authenticity of both passages; they are, in fact, an echo of our lives. Yet we find it hard to reconcile them. Why? Because we do not understand the nature of a strong father's love.

Only father and mother love together reveal to us the nature of God's love for us. A father's love not only gives us something; it makes us something. By leading us to growth, to responsibility, and to maturity, it continues the father's work of begetting us.

A mother's love has the ability to continue reaching out to her child no matter what he does, no matter how he degrades himself. An unfailing love, it reveals to us the sheer gift-character of God's love for us. It is a perpetual refuge from despair.

A father's love — no less true love — is expressed in a different way, a less tender way, a stronger way, and even (if this be possible) a still less selfless way. It is a pillar of support. It lifts us up. It refuses to accept us when we become what we are not — when we warp the image of the father in us. Yet like the father of the prodigal son, it never tires of waiting for us to return to our true selves.

A father's love has that great power of drawing us to become what we ought. A father's love is directed unerringly toward our real selves, never toward the false selves we sometimes become. It is a love filled with *authority* — that is, it is the love of an *author* of our being. The author has the right and the burden of working on his masterpiece faithfully to the end. He also must take responsibility for its effect upon others.

Thus it is that, both for the sake of the child and of the community where he will dwell, a father's love is demanding. It demands that the son honor the nobility of the self he has inherited from the father, and not despise himself by degrading himself. It demands that the son be a blessing and not a curse upon the community of men, lest the father be guilty of letting loose a menace upon others.

Faithful to these responsibilities, a father's love is strong enough to punish when correction is needed. Commenting on this matter, the author of the letter to the Hebrews wrote: "Have you forgotten that encouraging text in which you are addressed as sons? 'My son, when the Lord corrects you, do not treat it lightly; but do not get discouraged when He reprimands you. For the Lord trains the ones that He loves and He punishes all those that He acknowledges as His sons. Has there ever been any son whose father did not train Him? If you were not getting this training, as all of you are, then you would not be sons, but bastards.' "

Clearly, as indicated by this passage and by the quote from Jeremiah above, God will not be charmed by empty professions of love, or by fasts and sacrifices, into accepting the continuing evil conduct of His children.

Conversely, God the Father will not let the sacred cows of men stand in the way of what He wants to do for His children. This is clear from the Gospels. False interpretations of God's fatherly law of Sabbath rest could not resist Christ's will to heal the sick even on the Sabbath. With a strong love in the likeness of His Father's, Jesus swept aside the obstacles of false interpretation and did His work of healing.

A father's love is an undying passion to give life that goes on long after his child's birth. Often misunderstood in its purpose, often resented in its authority, it sweeps forward — undeterred by ingratitude — giving, forming, leading, infusing by guidance and punishment and attractively strong love the fullness of the life it began.

In the case of the highest Father, it is satisfied with nothing less than the ultimate goal: "You, therefore, must be perfect as your heavenly Father is perfect." That perfection consists in sharing the life the Father has given His only begotten Son.

"The whole creation," Paul wrote to the Romans, "is eagerly waiting for God to reveal His sons." We have a term to describe that moment of revelation. We call it the general resurrection.

In the meantime, we can say of any father (whether God the Father, the Holy Father, the priest, or the head of each family) — "His lot is not an easy one." Still, repayment comes from children like the little boy getting a haircut. "How do you want it?" the barber asked. "Just like Dad's," the boy proudly replied, "with a hole in the middle!"

2

The Young Will Be Free

The old man praised God and took into his arms the Child who would set men free. Hoary old Anna then appeared, to sing her prophetic praise for this Child of redemption.

In Simeon and Anna, Adam and Eve were casting their silhouettes across the ages. At long last, Adam could be heard laughing once more. Blackness was lifting, the ice was breaking up, lights were going on in the dungeons of man, and the chains were falling off, the shackles were breaking up.

Jesus brought into the world so many freedoms that no one has yet credited Him with them all, and in fact no one has yet known them all. They are still coming to light.

To know how much freedom Christ brought we have to look both backward and forward. Looking back, we find that Jesus came into a world loaded down with ignorance and superstition about God. Some peoples were adoring the natural elements, which God had given man to dominate from the beginning.

The Greeks and Romans peopled the heavens with gods and goddesses more depraved than their worshipers. Such gods gave more of an excuse for perversity than a mandate for sanctity. These man-made gods only herded men deeper into sin.

The Jews were free of idolatry, but they were slaves of the Old Law. The Law kept them from far worse slaveries, and it also served to make them cry out for a better delivery. It prepared them for Jesus.

Jesus set men free both of sin and of the Law which sin made necessary. Jesus Himself endured the slavery of the Law, thereby ending it forever.

Jesus Himself had to be circumcised, and keep the ritual feasts when He came of age, and participate in the Feast of the Paschal Lamb until the very year in which He became the Paschal Lamb.

That terrible moment in which Jesus would become the slain Lamb seems to be the very moment concerning which Simeon prophesied to Mary. It is the sign of death, contradicted by the resurrection. It is the sign of Easter, rejected by unbelievers. It is the sign of great suffering which pierced Mary's heart.

By sharing with man His divine sonship and its risen life, Jesus freed humanity in principle from all the fens and bogs of mental and spiritual enslavement. What this means is still coming to light.

The old generation (Simeon and Anna) amazed the intermediate generation (Joseph and Mary) by revealing great things about the youngest generation (the Child). How we need, today, wise old men and women who can see what God is working in the young and who can help to explain them to their parents in a way to inspire wonder and hope.

In the young today, God is continuing the work of Christ. He is continuing to promote the freedom of the children of God. What Jesus said and did on earth ended centuries ago. The effects of His works, however, are still coming to light one by one.

Instead of stupidly criticizing everything different as worse, we ought more often to stand reflectively, if not with bated breath, to try to understand what God is bringing about in our young people. If it is directly a result of what Christ has accomplished — of the Spirit of Sonship He has poured out — it deserves in some sense the title of ongoing revelation.

If we had sense enough to believe realistically what we claim we believe dogmatically, we would be much more open to a little of this wondering and watching. We would be a new kind of Jonah — happy Jonahs — sitting on the hillside, waiting for the transformation of man that must come about now that the alchemy of the new creation has been set bubbling within by the release of the spirit that makes us say, "Father!"

We Christians have ceased to live our own lives. We now live Christ's. We are no longer willing to be "stolid and stunned, the brother of the ox." With the nobility of the Son, we are through giving in to slavery. Is this not the Spirit sweeping irresistibly across the world?

We want the rights of the Son, and we want His inheritance. Even those who do not know why, can still be seen to have the Spirit of Jesus crying out in them "Abba!" and "Freedom!" and "Brotherhood!" and "Christ's inheritance over earth and heaven!"

We of the past generation of Christians did not adequately represent our hope in these things, or live them, or gain them. Then had we better not leave room for the children to find them as the Spirit is driving them?

If we could see with faith's eyes what God is working, we might well turn the future over to the children with hope in our hearts like that in Simeon's and Anna's.

When the Second Vatican Council came to a close, it addressed its final message to youth: "It is you who, receiving the best of the example of the teaching of your parents and teachers, are to form the society of tomorrow. You will either save yourselves or you will perish with it. . . . The Church looks to you with confidence and with love."

The message points out that it was above all for the sake of youth that the Church renewed herself. Her model is "the Christ who is eternally young."

The Council Fathers hope the young will do better than some of their elders in skirting the pitfalls of egoism, hedonism, and nihilism. They hope that "in the face of atheism, a phenomenon of lassitude and old age, you will know how to reaffirm your faith in life and in what gives meaning to life — that is to say, the certitude of the existence of a just and good God."

From earliest youth the sonly heart of Jesus aspired to greatness, and to win salvation for the farthest parts of the earth. This is a quality young people aspire to imitate, and the message to youth says: "Fight against all egoism. Refuse to give free course to the instincts of violence and hatred which beget wars and all their train of miseries. Be generous, pure, respectful and sincere, and build in enthusiasm a better world than your elders had."

Jesus' sonly heart also had an unheard-of capacity for self-effacing brotherliness. The night before He died He said: "Truly, truly I say to you, he who believes in me will also do the works that I do; and greater works than these will He do."

If the older generations could find it in their heart to uproot jealousy and say the same to their children, they would be worthy of the children they have generated, and they would have hope.

3

Family Life

A man who could heal the family could heal the world. The truth of this axiom should be self-evident. The family is father of the man, and society is made up of the men and women fed into it by its families.

If the world needs healing, it is because the family needs healing. The current earthquakes rocking human society are the totalizations of the change, unrest and strife within the basic building block of society, the family.

The revelation that came through Jesus and Mary has power to heal the human family. The Gospel episode of the misunderstanding within the Holy Family sheds light on what Christian families can expect and on what they ought to do to profit by the family life of Jesus, Mary, and Joseph.

The episode began as a happy family venture. Jesus, now twelve, traveled to Jerusalem with His parents to celebrate the passover from slavery to freedom. When the time came to return home, the Boy remained behind with no explanation — or at least none that His parents had grasped.

When at last His parents found Him, Mary confronted her Son with the anguished question: *Why?*

The question has never really been answered. The Boy Jesus gave an answer, but anyone who could understand the answer would never have asked the question: "Why were you looking for Me? Did you not know I must be busy with My Father's affairs?"

I think that by reflecting we can come to understand this answer. I think Mary did, eventually. I don't think this episode was a unique one. I think it must have been followed by many similar episodes in the course of Jesus' family life, episodes that kept revealing to Joseph and Mary the true nature of family life.

Think of Jesus as He matured and worked in Nazareth. His heart would have gone out to the poor and underprivileged He met. And they would have found Him, they would have glued themselves to Him and eaten their way into His life, and claimed Him as their belonging.

Jesus may have run His own carpenter shop. How did He keep solvent? Soon every pauper would have become His customer.

Yes, but did not Jesus have to care for His own family first? Ah, there is the question which Jesus makes every man answer. Jesus once compelled His listeners to formulate an even more basic question: "And who is my neighbor?" We know the answer to that question. *Or do we?*

We cannot know the answer to that question until we know the answer to another question which is involved in it: *And who is my family?*

How do we answer that question? For one thing, the parents and the children are answering it in different ways today. Parents think they owe everything to their children and little to the children of others. They give their children all they can and sicken their own children with their smothering selfishness. If they gave half as much to their own children and twice as much to the children of others, they would give ten times as much to their own children and win their hearts by doing it.

Children have been born into a new world crammed together by an electronic nervous system. Every child is their neighbor and their brother. *This has got to mean something in the way we live as families.*

Once when Jesus' relatives were laying a claim on Him He asked: "Who is My mother? Who are My brothers?" And He answered: "Anyone who does the will of My Father in heaven, he is My brother and sister and mother."

Once we really see God as Father of all flesh, our vision expands and our responsibilities shift. Family walls dilate, and we are enriched and burdened with the family of man.

This truth would be more readily absorbed if we ever really learned that motherhood is for the sake of the child, not of the mother. Parenthood is for the sake of the children, not of the parents. The great households of old in which parents ruled their children and their children's children as kings ruled subjects and slaves is only a memory in the West. Even in the East it is crashing to the ground. Never did parenthood demand a more selfless heart.

Parents who achieve this selflessness with their own children open their hearts readily to all children and to all families. They see the limits of family claims, for we all belong to all. Jesus was not unique in this. He called Himself our Way.

Priestly and religious celibacy is only symbolic of what every Christian ought to be — open to all, belonging to all. We must all die to our own families to really possess them, because we cannot possess even our own families unless we have embraced all families meaningfully. If I do not care what happens to someone else's brother, then I really do not care what happens to my own brother except that he is *mine*. In that case, it is not what he is in himself, but what he is to me that counts. And that is mere selfishness and fleshiness, not love of the other for his own sake.

Jesus translated divine family life into human terms, and Jesus and Mary and Joseph made new breakthroughs in interpreting family life and relating it to the lives of other families.

Mary's Son had forever known the divine Trinitarian life where all is fulfillment, and yet He had been willing to come forth from it into our emptiness to share Himself with us. Is it any wonder then that He also had to burst the limits of Mary's family circle and let in a flood of life from the whole world through the gap He opened by going forth to the world? Mary had to learn to be the mother of all the living. So must every mother and father; and every child must be sibling to all children. This is what it means to be about our Father's business, for the business of our Father is the life of all the living.

If the human situation is so tragedy-prone that dialogue could momentarily break down between this sinless Son and Mother, then how obvious is the need to make every effort at communication in families where ordinary human selfishness prevails?

Jesus and Mary profited from this heartbreaking misunderstanding. Jesus grew in wisdom; Mary listened to what her young Son had to say, and kept thinking about it, and she too learned.

The call to discuss things with the children is not a call to weaken authority. Authority is responsibility for guidance. The responsibility cannot be lived up to except through efforts to understand those to be guided. Good communications make obedience less strained. The Boy Jesus went home "and was obedient."

4

The Marriage Parable

"When," Timmy asked his friend Tommy, "is your sister thinking of getting married?" "Constantly!" Tommy replied.

Tommy's sister has good company. From the first chapters of the Bible, through most of the Greek myths, to the latest novels, we find mankind intent on the search for a glorious love.

According to the wisdom of the myths, man needs woman's beauty, affection, and fruitfulness, while woman needs man's strength, devotion, and service.

The biblical Song of Songs is an eternal paean to the love of man and woman. Clearly and ringingly it sounds the triumph of love over all else: "Were a man to offer all the wealth of his house to buy love, contempt is all he would purchase."

In the second chapter of John's Gospel we find Jesus enjoying a wedding festival, and Mary calling upon Him to ensure its success.

Well might Jesus seek to ensure the success of all weddings and all marriages! Jesus' mission was to multiply man's blessings, and marriage is for the vast majority of human beings the way to contentment through human love, and the way to perfection, which is perfect love of God.

Too long ignored is God's invitation calling all men to sanctity and to sainthood, whatever their state of life. It is in fact unthinkable that the Maker of man should make for man and woman a compelling state of union that would in any way exclude them from perfect love of Himself.

"Be perfect," Christ said to all, "as your heavenly Father is perfect." Similarly, Paul told the Ephesians that the God and Father of our Lord Jesus Christ "chose us in Christ before the foundation of the world that we should be holy and blameless before Him." And in his letter to the Romans Paul indiscriminately calls all Christians "saints," because that is what they are called to be in the blood of Christ.

This calling on everyone to share in Christ's perfect holiness is taught by the Council in its Constitution on the Church: "Christ, the Son of God, who with the Father and the Spirit is praised as being 'alone holy,' loved the Church as His Bride, delivering Himself up for her. This He did that He might sanctify her. He united her to Himself as His own body and crowned her with the gift of the Holy Spirit, for God's glory. Therefore in the Church, everyone belonging to the hierarchy, or being cared for by it, is called to holiness, according to the saying of the Apostle: 'For this is the will of God, your sanctification.' "

Catholic couples need the illumination and the strength that comes from the awareness of their call to holiness. It fortifies them and motivates them to carry on when they discover they have embraced a state of life which is full not only of great joys but of great hardships. Most couples would much more readily bear the outrages of life if they understood the greatness that is at stake in these events, because through them they can extend Christ's victory of love over self and life over death.

It is this realistic concept of marriage that prompts the Church to make the bridegroom and then the bride say: "I (name) take you (name) for my lawful wife, to have and to hold, from this day forward, for better, for worse, for richer, for poorer, in sickness and in health, until death do us part."

The bridal pair are told that our Savior has transformed marriage, "giving it a character of sanctity which places it among the holiest institutions of religion." Christ did this to join the couple to

Himself, but also to fortify them in overcoming all obstacles to their earthly and eternal happiness.

Human nature has been seared by the selfishness of sin, and only a return to the holiness-meaning of marriage can give families the strength and generous love they need to belong to one another selflessly. Married happiness depends on living the married life according to the nature God gave it and the mysterious new dimensions Christ added.

God made marriage as an image of His own communitarian life. "In the image of God He made him; male and female He made them." Marriage is, therefore, a parable of God. *The couple reveal God to one another and to the children.*

Marriage is also a parable of Christ. Paul wrote of the marriage union: "This mystery has many implications; but I am saying it applies to Christ and the Church."

Gravest of all dangers to marriage is that of apotheosizing the marriage by excluding God. Genesis records our protoparents' sin of shutting God out to give superiority to their own mutuality. Since marriage is founded on God, sins against marriage undermine its foundations.

Mary's unique role in marriage teaches and restores divine primacy. When Mary bore her Child, she shared the Child with her husband Joseph, but she shared Him even more with His Father, God.

God is jealous of His fatherhood in the birth of every child. "Call no man your father on earth, for you have one Father, who is in heaven."

God is jealous of His primacy in every wedding. He is first Lord and first Love of both members of the wedding. His covenant love in both Old and New Testaments is superior to the covenant love between man and woman. Their lovely covenant love is a parable of the love to which they are both called in Christ. It mirrors, too, the eternal Trinity's covenant love.

Meditation on these mysteries can be for married couples a deeper draft of the wine of Christ's love and of marriage love than was provided for the wedding in Cana.

5

Youth Feel Betrayed

St. Paul warned the young Timothy that a time would come when men "will hold to the outward form of religion, but reject its real power." Many of the young today think that their culture, their teachers, and their own Christian parents are showing these false signs of religion.

Television insinuates that happiness is a new hairspray, and peace two aspirin tablets. Parents think worship of God consists in a service on Sunday and a tight little system of closed morality during the week — a morality in which you take care of your own little circle and let the rest of the world go to hell.

Educators cram youth with a phenomenal outpouring of facts — and reveal by their own conduct that they have no lesson to teach about the meaning of life. Parents entrust the impressionable minds of their children to amoral teachers whom they wouldn't trust in a business deal.

Young people want liturgy and personal morality to produce social results, or it is nothing to them but another form of self-seeking. And they are right. The commandments are for the sake of love. Examine them and see.

They expect people who profess religion to show concern for

religious responsibilities. They look to see how you react to the need of the black to be human and of the Vietnamese to be peaceful and the Biafran to have bread because it means life.

They watch to see whether you resort to force or justice to bring order. They observe you sitting complacently by while the foreign aid program shrinks year by year, though people are still crushed to the earth by inhuman poverty in any international direction you refuse to look.

They are clever in cutting through sham cults and exposing the bowels of hypocrisy. In their own language, they vomit at what people do and grace with the euphemism, "religion." Like the protagonist of "The Graduate," they may turn out even more depraved themselves, but they plan to blame it on you.

The various youth protests are rebellions against the vapid system of life-values foisted on the young today by their culture, their educators, and even their Christian parents. One of the greatest deterrents to a dedicated life today are the many Catholic parents who treat a boy wishing to become a priest as if he were immature, and a girl who wishes to become a nun as if she were crazy.

Yet the star of the true meaning of man did shoot up irresistibly over Bethlehem, and it still leads wise men there to discover themselves by discovering Christ.

Christ impatiently sweeps away all bickering about life and gives us life's meaning. He imperiously sweeps away all arguments about authority and reveals life's master.

"You shall love the Lord your God," He says, "with all your heart, with all your soul, and with all your mind. This is the greatest and the first commandment. And the second is similar to it. You shall love your neighbor as yourself."

Here is the meaning of man and of life. Life is not found in accumulating things, but in joining the web of all other lives by an outpouring of love and service.

At the heart of that network of lives is Jesus Christ, its vital center. Jesus points that out too. He explains that when the ancient King David, in prophecy, called the future Messiah "Lord," he was revealing by the power of the Spirit that this future member of his clan was more than merely another king like himself. He was, through some great mystery, to be Lord like the Lord God.

The young know that Christianity teaches this. But do they have parents and priests who can say to them what Paul said to Timothy: "You have followed my teaching, my conduct, and my purpose in life; you have observed my faith, my patience, my love, my endurance, my persecutions and my sufferings"? In other words, do they have men and women they can follow and not simply listen to?

The young are hungry for heroes of love but can't find them. They are yearning to follow the true Lord, but who is leading the way with enough passion and ardor to win their admiration?

Disillusioned, they set out to find the way themselves, without much of a compass. They blunder into hippydom and yippydom, and begin to disintegrate, but not without first giving witness against the materialism and the selfishness they have rejected at great cost to themselves, and not without giving meaningful signs of their own genuine aspirations.

"I never thought I would see the day when I would take to a platform to praise the hippies," said James M. Norris, assistant to the executive director of Catholic Relief Services; "but every day they walk into our New York offices, complete with long beards, and give us money they have raised for Biafra."

Youthful judgments can be cruel and unjust. They demand of their leaders more than flesh and blood can give. To lead nevertheless is our responsibility. But if we fail them Christ will not. He will continue to offer those young enough to be hungry for heroism the call to break away from trivial and unfaithful living and follow Him.

6

Companionship

General Sheridan in powwow with Indians was trying to show the futility of fighting the white man. He described the white man's big iron horses belching fire and the immense war canoes rowed by steam, but the interpreter reported: "General, they don't believe you!" Thinking of the newly invented telephone, the general told how he could talk through a black box to the "great white father" in distant Washington and hear him answer at once. "General," drawled the interpreter, "now I don't believe you!"

Our Christian faith embraces a great mystery we have grown accustomed to believing, the mystery of the most Blessed Trinity. We turn to it because our love of God yearns to know Him; it searches out "even the deep things of God."

The pondering of the mystery of the Trinity is supremely rewarding because this mystery holds the content of Christianity and the meaning of life.

"How unsearchable His ways!" cries St. Paul in his letter to the Romans. Paul is not telling us we can know nothing about the mystery of God, but only that we can never know everything.

Jesus is the great revelation of the Trinity. To Thomas Jesus said: "If you know Me you know My Father also. From this moment you know Him and have seen Him." Philip pursued the point: "Lord, show us the Father." Jesus answered with distress: "Have I been with you all this time, Philip, and you still do not know Me? To have seen Me is to have seen the Father. . . . You must believe Me when I say that I am in the Father, and the Father is in Me."

This is the answer to the ancient Greek philosopher who pitied God because He alone lacked all companionship. From all eternity the first divine Person produced a divine likeness of Himself who is called the Logos (Word), or Wisdom, or Beauty, or Son, or, in His Incarnation, Jesus.

Jesus further reveals that the Father and the Son's mutual Holiness, their mutual Truthfulness, their mutual Love, is Personal, is a Person. He is called Love; He is called mutual Gift. Saints have called Him the "Kiss" of the first two divine Persons.

See what this means. It means that company is more than two, and three is not a crowd. Love is fecund, and love that is not is failed love. Love can give the mortal and spiritual life wedded Christians give their children, or it can give the spiritual life which the celibate priest gives to a host of children. For by its nature, which comes down from the Trinity, love is "a sacrifice on behalf of life." Love is "a flash of fire, a flame of God Himself," and God is Life and Lifegiver.

This mysterious divine Community is not really so strange to mankind. Concerning man Scripture says: "In the image of God He created him; male and female He created them." And Pope Paul said: "In the divine and mysterious persons the essence and the relations are profoundly identical. Each person is an eternal gift and thus man and woman, created in resemblance to, in the image of, the Trinity, are called upon by that resemblance to give themselves mutually to one another."

Marriage and family are God, written small. "By marriage and the family," Pope Paul added, ". . . God has wisely joined two of the greatest human realities: the mission to transmit life and the love of man and woman."

We were created in the likeness of the Trinity, but salvation is more. Salvation is participation not only in the likeness but in the life of the Trinity. Baptism is the ingress. "Go, therefore," Jesus commands us, "and make disciples of all nations by baptizing them in the name of the Father and of the Son and of the Holy Spirit."

The knowledge and love of the Trinity which we gain through faith and baptism *is* life. "Eternal life is this," said Jesus, "to know You, the only God, and Jesus Christ whom You have sent."

The enjoyment of this fellowship has already begun: "If anyone loves Me he will keep My word," Jesus said, "and My Father will love him, and we will come to him and make our home with him."

The Spirit of Love, too, is our companion, as these words of Jesus to the Father make clear: "I have made Your name known to them, and will continue to make it known, so that the love with which You loved Me may be in them, and so that I may be in them."

This fellowship unites us in the Trinity itself: "May they all be one, Father," Jesus prayed; "may they be one in us, as You are in Me and I am in You." It is, however, the Eucharist more than baptism which is productive of union in one life: "As I . . . Myself draw life from the Father," Jesus said, "so whoever eats Me will draw life from Me."

It is, according to the author of Hebrews, through the pierced side of the risen Jesus that we must enter into the mystery and the life of the divine Trinity. That is why the liturgical feast of the Blessed Trinity is followed closely by the feast of the Blessed Sacrament.

Those who feast mysteriously on the Eucharist will one day feast openly with the Three who are now so mysterious. When they do, it will be something given, not something earned. "Were a man to offer all the wealth of his house to buy love," observes the Song of Songs, "contempt is all he would purchase." God is not for sale. The Trinity is a free Gift to their loved ones.

7

A Pattern for Personhood

"The younger generation is the pet set dedicated to criticizing the older generation's accomplishments." Why? Strangely enough, it is a matter of love and likeness.

To build, man needs a pattern. One of my earliest memories is of my mother cutting cloth from a full-scale paper pattern. Later, I saw my father studying blueprints. Later still I pored over schematics for countless hours to render intelligible the jungle of wires inhabiting the chassis of some electronic instrument. We can't act intelligently without a plan or a pattern.

What then of the project of building a man? What of the difficulty of threading one's way out of the maze of adolescence into adulthood? Is it any wonder little boys march around with gigantic steps in imitation of their fathers? Or that little girls clack about the house in their mothers' shoes? Or that teen-agers grow bitter and caustically criticize parents who are inadequate patterns? What can the young mariners do to set their course when the compass breaks and the stars go out in the heavens?

The most profound psychological and philosophical studies only confirm our need for the model or ideal of what we are to become. Some living things have inbuilt patterns, but not man.

Acorns germinate and spring into full-blown oak trees without guidance from anyone. But a child who grows like topsy will look topsy-turvy when grown.

Karl Jung has shown that the child identifies almost mystically with the deepest emotional life and hidden drives and desires of his parents. Not merely what he sees, but the electric tensions of the parental psychic life he feels and senses are his pattern. To build himself into a son of man, a child needs his parents, both parents.

Christ carries us higher still in the scale of life. He sets before us the individual and communal project of building ourselves into children of God: "All who are led by the Spirit of God are sons of God." The Spirit of the Son of God came at baptism to be the power within by which we are growing into the children of God.

This growth into divine sonship involves not only God's work but our free and intelligent cooperation. To cooperate, we need a pattern before our eyes and our mind. The sole pattern that will do is Jesus.

"In your minds you must be the same as Christ Jesus," Paul wrote to the Philippians; "His state was divine, yet He did not cling to His equality with God, but emptied Himself to assume the condition of a slave, and become as men are; and being as all men are, He was humbler still, even to accepting death, death on a cross."

Jesus, true-born Son of God, became also "the Son of Man" by His birth from a woman. In His humanity, He is the one pattern for us all. *He is the finite version of God.*

Jesus was always true Son of God and true Brother of us all. He sided with God in every dispute between God and man. He not only showed a Son's obedient love in doing this, but He manifested His faithfulness to us. Only a faithful son of God is a true brother to anyone. By love Jesus identified with the Father in His heart, and by obedience He identified with the Father in action.

"The Son does nothing except what He sees the Father do," Jesus said. The Father is the sole pattern for the Son, as the Son is the only pattern for all of us who want to share in His divine sonship.

Jesus radiates the force of mature personality without ever ceasing to be filial and creaturely in His humanity. No one was as aware as He that to be fully human is to be by definition dependent.

Despite His religious intensity, Jesus was never a religious fanatic. He was a genuinely human person who loved all the things of earth. He loved especially the ordinary little things of life, which crop up so richly in His parables. Farmers and housewives, seeds and brooms and cattle, lamps and clothes, wine and banquets and wedding feasts all parade by to give us a faithful image of the life of His times.

Jesus' prudence was profound, but it was never a disguise for "safeness" or "cowardice." It was putting first things first: "Give to Caesar what is Caesar's, and to God what is God's."

Jesus rejected violent means to bring about human brotherhood. Violence breeds violence. Violence presupposes enemies, and brotherhood denies we have enemies. It admits only that we are at enmity with the evil in our brothers — as well as in ourselves; and it counsels us to root out the evil and not the brother, for certainly we do not destroy *ourselves* to destroy the evil in us.

Jesus sets the pattern of filial love and brotherly affection. He first lived it, then He taught it. When He taught, He put His likeness into words. His teaching is a picture of Himself.

Realist that He is, Jesus provided, in the parable of the dishonest steward, a minimal pattern of salvation for our days of weakness. If we won't be kind to others out of brotherly love, He is saying, we ought at least to be kind to save our own skins.

That is at least self-love, and self-love is a beginning. If a son does not love himself, he will love no one, neither man nor God. If he loves himself, there is hope he will come to love both God and man, when he discovers he is made in their likeness.

God the Father has been kind to us. He has given us not only the highest of calls, but the most perfect of patterns in fulfillment of our call. Jesus our pattern is no dead letter but a living person communicating with us in prayer and sacrament. Our Way abides with us.

8

The Human Jesus

God's love always comes to us as a person. On a certain day in Bethlehem, the person who came in love was God Himself. Persons who bring love into our lives arrive in many ways. On that day, the way was by birth.

We Christians love very much the birthday feast of our Lord and Savior Jesus Christ. If we compare it with Easter, we readily observe that the feast of His Nativity warms our hearts more. Yet is not Easter the day that man first went home to God? Yes, but Christmas is the day God first came home to us.

The angel announced to the shepherds a sign of Jesus' arrival that is deeply appealing to us today: "You will find an infant wrapped in swaddling clothes and laid in a manger." The Greek word which the Jerusalem Bible translates as "manger" also means a stable, an animal's stall, or a feeding place under the open sky. It is by such details as these that the Evangelists bring home to us the humanness of Jesus.

We are intensely interested in the humanness of Jesus because we first believe in His divineness. We Catholics have so jealously and triumphantly guarded our faith in the divinity of Jesus that our good sense regarding His humanness has been blurred. Reflection on His Nativity is one way to help us come back into focus.

Our problem of knowing Jesus is just the reverse of the problem facing those who lived with Him. From our own infancy we are taught that Jesus is God, and the very glow of our faith obscures our awareness of how genuinely human Jesus is. His contemporaries, on the other hand, had no trouble at all recognizing Him as a man. We have to discover His humanity, but they had to discover His divinity.

Mary and Joseph saw that Jesus was flesh of our flesh in the moment of His birth. Mary had to nurse Him, wash Him, cuddle Him when He cried.

Jesus was "Son of Man." He had all the human experiences, except sin, for the good reason that His humanity was identically like ours. While a little boy, He enjoyed playing as all little boys do. As He grew He experienced the mysterious physical and psychological changes with which every teen-ager wrestles.

He knew what it was to be warmed by a kiss. He complained once because He was not kissed. He may have fallen in love with some village girl, though He would not tell her because His plans and labors for universal salvation of the race excluded personal marriage to one woman.

No doubt He enjoyed His mother's good cooking. He said Himself that He came eating and drinking.

He shared all the joys and sorrows of our own family lives. More than once He must have been touched by some indisposition of His mother. He probably wept at His foster father's grave.

Jesus had special gifts of knowledge to help Him in His work, but some scriptural exegetes feel that believers have falsely exaggerated Jesus' human knowledge to the point of dehumanizing Him.

If Jesus was genuinely tempted, if He had disappointments, if He had to make plans and change them when men refused cooperation, then in some sense He, like us, did not know what the morrow would bring.

Jesus embraced these limitations for us but we, in a false show of honor, ascribe to Him human knowledge which Scripture seems to show He did not have. Aware of His divinity, we try to make of His manhood a superman.

In doing this, we undo God's work. We undermine our own

belief that God's only begotten Son genuinely assumed our human condition. We undermine our hope of living in His image and likeness, and we discount our solemn obligation of doing it. We make it look as though we cannot live like Him, yet He said we can and must.

Thinking about Jesus' birthday invites us to renew our quest for the human Jesus. There are ways of discovering His humanity for ourselves. The Gospels tell us much about it, if we read them reflectively. Better still, we use our imagination in prayer. We join Mary and Joseph at the birth of Jesus. With the help of Scripture, we picture for ourselves how things must have been. Again, by the power of the imagination, we accompany the disciples on their journeys with Jesus. By the use of their memoirs, we experience secondhand what they lived out firsthand.

We learn of Jesus in another important way. We meet Jesus personally in the sacraments, especially the Eucharist. Jesus was laid in a feeding place from the beginning to make it known that now the true Bread of Heaven has fallen to earth. God's Bread is living, personal, human, self-disclosing. People of strong faith come to know Jesus as personally as did the Apostles.

All the great myths of human love are outdistanced by the reality of Christmas. Across 2,000 years, Christians have believed in God's great love journey down into our flesh, and some have responded in kind. They have gone penniless, unmarried, persecuted. They have borne the burdens of parenthood to give birth to His members. They have served without measuring any cost, they have burned with love for the God who visited us in the flesh.

They have appreciated the fact that Jesus has made all our human actions more holy, more divine — *and more human than ever.* Yet love of the Word made Flesh draws them up to love of things unseen, and makes earth an exile until their homecoming.

9

Conquest of Temptation

Enemies of biological life run the gamut from swarming microbes to raging lions. Survival requires more vitality and determination than that characteristic of these agents of death.

Moral life and spiritual life have their own kinds of mortal enemies. Refusal to battle means inner death long before outer dissolution sets in.

Life is a series of struggles to make decisions that guard and enhance the worth of life. The man who evades decisions drifts with the tides. He ends up with the flotsam and jetsam of life.

Jesus struggled in the desert to define His messianic role. He struggled against His people's materialistic concept of life. Should He bring them what they wanted or what they needed?

Should He bring them growing life with all its growing pains and struggles, or merely the inert materials of affluence on which life can be squandered? Was nobility to be measured by vain honors or by the struggle to adhere to true life? Was freedom to be the law of license or the law of finite love lived out in the likeness of the Father's Incarnate Word?

Jesus rose up against the enticement of the false answers and hewed the false ways to bits with the word of God for His sword.

Now it is our turn. Fathers, mothers, children, and all Christians are compelled by Christ's example to reexamine their own lives. We cannot take our direction from our peer group or the muddied path of the herd. Faith and conscience light the way for the only valid decisions.

Every father must face questions similar to those which confronted Jesus. What is true life and true fatherhood? Is the center of a father's life his career or his family? Is it more important that he give his family his wages or himself? Both are necessary, but which has priority? Which should control the shape of his life?

Every mother faces similar questions. What is her most important gift: her services or her affections? Is she to explode every time her labors are undone by carelessly muddy feet or thoughtless tardiness at meals? Is the object of her attentions an orderly home or a happy home?

Does she budget in such a way as to provide everything needed around the house except peace of mind? Does she goad her husband to the conclusion that to bring home a bigger paycheck is more important than to bring himself home? Does she promote his moonlighting absenteeism, with the result that she robs her children of life's true riches, a contented mother and an available father?

The children have their own decisions to make. Are they supposed to nag good parents for permissions reasonably refused on the pretext that "everybody's doing it"? That excuse is not potent enough to delude a good adolescent mind. It is dishonest and irrelevant except for the flotsam and the jetsam.

To be men and women we must make our decisions about life; but decisions are futile unless we execute them. The effort to carry out our decisions is not uncommonly as beset by struggles as were the decisions themselves. That is why the determinations Jesus made in the desert eventually had to be confirmed during a bloody sweat in Gethsemane.

There are ways to overcome the temptations, and even compulsive habits of sin, which may be blocking the execution of our decisions. But these ways are not cheap. They cannot be bought with a mere act of the will. They involve an outlay of time and effort and energy.

The first means to fidelity is to deepen our knowledge and love of God. Great love of God automatically frees us from enslavement to non-gods. Since "no man has seen God" except in Jesus, the project is one of getting to know Jesus through prayer, the Eucharist, the Gospels, and through the service of other men made in His likeness.

The second means of overcoming temptation is a properly Christian hope of success, and a genuine readiness to take the means to success. Success in overcoming sin is guaranteed the Christian by Scripture. "How can we who died to sin still live in it?" Paul demands to know. Any serious sin after baptism is a deliberate turning away from Christ our life to false life. *What is not deliberate is not a sin. What is deliberate can be changed.*

We must, nevertheless, have genuine readiness to take the means to success. We must have this attitude (which all winners have in every field): "Only when I have taken the means that work, have I taken means enough."

The third means is to admit the fault to someone (if that would not be imprudent). For the Catholic, this means confession. Confession makes the admission to both God and man, and wins forgiveness and help from both God and His Church. Frequent confession is one of the great means to integrity.

The fourth means is to use not only our will but our intelligence in the service of moral and spiritual victories. Any military general who has lost a battle through a faulty plan or an unfortunate choice of terrain will never use that plan again or be caught deployed on that terrain. Translated, this means we must apply our problem-solving skills to our spiritual warfare. In battling temptation, it is always possible to change some circumstance, and practically always necessary. Endless variations in strategy and tactics can be employed until the victory is won.

A fifth means to overcoming temptation is the good sense to find pleasure, recreation and relaxation in appropriate and healthy ways. Every effort to preserve a happy marriage is priceless insurance against marital infidelity. People who are constantly nagging one another do not need a confessor; they need a vacation.

A sixth means is a daily examination of conscience. Without this any temporary victory will soon be dissipated by a drift back into the former morass. The last state may be worse than the first.

A final means (insurance against discouragement) is to remember that no temptation is useless, and no struggle goes unrewarded. When the Chinese shelled Quemoy and Matsu, they meant the shelling to be a rain of death. Yet after each barrage the poor people rushed out, collected the spent shells, and sold them to support life.

With every temptation permitted, God gives both a way out and a way to profit. We sometimes need ingenuity to find either or both. But they are there. "To them that love God," Paul wrote, "all things work together unto good."

Life is a struggle against many enemies, but God is the one ally who outnumbers them all. In their many battles for freedom, the Maccabees adopted the watchword: "Victory from God." And they did, in fact, win great victories. For Christians, Christ has appointed the watchword for the greatest victory of all: "Fear not, for I have overcome the world."

10

The Service of Life

Generosity not corroded by self-interest is so rare that men pry for self-serving motives behind even the noblest services. Service of others must be genuinely selfless, humble and brotherly. If it is done for an ulterior motive, or infested with arrogance, it is service of the self.

The actions which we do for others, like those which we do for ourselves, are done in the service of life. They give life, or heal it, augment it, and enhance it.

Jesus once said, "I have come that they may have life." And His life was spent in the service of life. His is the service we are called to imitate.

It would be hard to find a more touching service to life than the one Jesus rendered the bereaved widow. The village of Nain where Jesus met the widow in the funeral cortege with her dead son may be the modern village of Nein, near Jerusalem. Husbandless, the widow wept by the corpse of her only son. Not a service of superiority but immediate companionship in grief was the first service Jesus offered her.

Out of His service of compassion His service of lifegiving flowed: "Young man, I bid you rise up!" And the young man arose.

The God made known to us in the Judaeo-Christian tradition was always the Servant of widows and orphans. Through the godly men who are His stand-ins on earth He cared for them.

What then of the women bereaved in today's world? Clearly, they must be served by us. Not only the widows and the orphans, but every family with a father unable for any reason to support them needs our help.

The Decree on the Apostolate of the Laity urges laymen to extend help in the family area. It urges "support of married couples and families involved in material and moral crises." Now that parish councils are flourishing, direct interfamily help within the parish hopefully will flourish with them.

How important this is can be seen when one reflects that families are not only the building blocks of love which constitute society, but the centers of life which do by nature what Jesus did beyond nature: give life.

St. Paul cautions us, however, not to be so indiscreet in helping others in need or temptation that we fall into the same pit ourselves. It seems a fact, for instance, that quite a few priests who abandon their vocation often begin simply by helping a woman in need, but in indiscreet ways.

Mahatma Gandhi recounts a youthful effort to straighten out a wayward friend that accomplished nothing but to lead Gandhi to the brink of moral disaster. He concluded: "I am of the opinion that all exclusive intimacies are to be avoided; for man far more readily takes in vice than virtue. And he who would be friends with God must remain alone or make the whole world his friend."

The raising of the widow's son is reminiscent of the miraculous raising of a little boy from the dead by the prophet Elisha (2 Kings 4:35). It leads the people to realize that in Jesus "a great prophet has risen among us."

Jesus' service of giving life was thus also a sign — a sign and a promise of a greater gift of life to come. It foretells the life that was to be given another widow's Son on the first Easter, and through His risen life not only the Son but the widow and all the sons of men have the opportunity to be lifted to life everlasting.

The purpose of Christ's coming was to clear a way to life without mortal limits through the mystery of resurrection. We ought to rejoice frequently in our pledged resurrection, for only those who firmly realize the future is stored away for them by Christ are likely to take the means of preventing it from being plundered by false ways and false prophets. We have too much at stake to be gullible.

Stress on the resurrection is the authentic Christian emphasis. From the beginning the Apostles considered themselves appointed to be "the witnesses of the resurrection."

The priest, by the faith passed on to him and the hierarchic post appointed him in holy orders, has been delegated to carry on officially the witness to the resurrection. All Christians share with him this function according to the strength of their faith and the unselfishness of their lives.

The priest does more than give witness to the future life. He fathers it in Christ. By baptism and the Eucharist he communicates life, and by the sacrament of penance he restores it to man's spirit. All Christians, to the extent they die to selfishness and live for others, spread the Christ-life, and renew the world in Him.

Men and women who work in home or industry with love and selflessness collect two pays. The one comes at the end of the week. The other comes at the end-time. It is life.

11

Faith in Faith

One of the roots out of which the great human anguish of our day mushrooms is the problem of religious faith. Why does the hidden God expect such great faith of us? Why does He demand faith at all? Why not just *show us His face,* as Moses pleaded?

Some men would confine to two the possible answers. *Either there is no God,* they would say, *or He is playing at charades with us.* Since the second alternative is preposterous, they can do nothing but have recourse to atheism.

Why do we Christians conclude that both alternatives are wrong, that there is a third explanation behind the need for faith? We must go to history for the answer, because our God and our faith come to us out of history. But we must also go to man and to *love* for the answer, for it is not the nature of God alone that underlies the need of faith, but the nature of pilgrim man and of mysterious love.

What is man? Man tried to answer this question for himself in the course of time. He kept groping in the metaphysical darkness for his meaning. To this day philosophers are still searching.

Wise men did discover that all finite beings float in timeless seas of infinity. Mystery is the heritage of finitude. And the smog of sin darkens the darkness. Thus stand the human efforts to shed light on the mystery of man.

Long ago, however, a radiance beyond human making burst into history. It took the form of guidance: "Leave your country and your family and your father's house for the land I will show you." *It took the form of miracle and prophecy, and of a cloud of mystery.*

He who is, portrayed Himself as a mystery. Though He stood by His people in the course of events with unflagging manifestations of fidelity and love, He Himself remained cryptically inaccessible.

Why? Why come on the scene only to remain hidden? He Himself promises that in our final relations with Him "we shall see face to face." *Why not now?*

Perhaps the best answer to that question is the attitude of the ancients. They *feared* to see God's face lest they be disintegrated by the impact of the burst of His glory. Their reverence condemns our presumption. Arrogance asks God, "Why not now?" Humility says, "Why so mindful of man that one day You will even show us Your face?"

Not satisfied with this, we discover two avenues by which we can enter more deeply into the mystery: the phenomenon of man's natural growth, and the mystery of even human relationships.

Man, in both the individual and the species, rises up out of primeval weakness and self-darkness into the light and power of adulthood and civilization. In his better moments he doesn't ask why this should be so because he realizes there is a glory in what he is doing. He has been created to be a creator. His most marvelous product is himself. He is the helpmate of God in the human self-making project that will have as its *finale* entrance into the vision of God.

If natural growth and development make sense, why be confounded by the spiritual evolution wherein man spirals upward along an ascent clouded with the mystery of faith until he bursts out into the sunlight of the vision of God?

Human interpersonal relationships also shed light on the faith-relationship of man with God. Two persons meet in friendship and love, and from the seedling stages of their relationship only mutual faith provides the conditions of growth. We see one another's faces, but never those inner depths, those profoundly veiled conscious, subconscious and unconscious psychic "faces" partly or wholly mysterious even to their possessors. Not only must we believe in one another when we love, but we must believe first in ourselves, so pervasive is the mystery of faith.

When the Other is God, the frontiers of the mystery of person impinging upon person are yet more indefinable, for not even the first Face of God is discernible. Yet in many ways the event is like that of any two persons forming a friendship. There are self-revealing words and actions that profess fidelity and love. These arouse trust and a return of love. And so the ascent into those eternal realms of love and togetherness begins.

In all friendships there is some mutual transformation. *In friendship with God, the human friend is destined for a total transformation that will transmute him into the spiritual substance that gives him enough likeness to God to see Him.* The final stage of that transmutation occurs beyond history.

Parallel to these reasons runs another tributary of causes why God comes to us in faith. Briefly, He wants us to find and love Him in His creation. That is why His self-revelation was made to come to its term in the man Jesus. At one stroke Jesus reveals to man both man and God. For the man who discovers Jesus not only at long last discovers himself, but "He who sees Me sees also the Father."

Faith is, then, the normal, tender beginnings of friendship with God. It even shows the normal fluctuations of dawning love, which "never runs smooth." Need often paves the way to faith, as with the royal official in the fourth chapter of John. He asked the cure of his son, and received together with it sight for his soul.

Life's universal law is that evil must be suppressed and good propagated. It is no different with faith. The royal official immediately lit up his whole household with the fire of his faith. The Apostles "preached the message of truth and begot Churches." Those who give the faith to others keep it most firmly themselves. Faith remains healthy only when it remains fruitful.

PART TWO

12

The Battle of Faith

Why do men unnecessarily complicate the problem of faith by deliberately interposing obstacles to God's revelation? That they do interpose such obstacles is attested to by St. John's Gospel.

John captures the drama of Christ in conflict with men who obstinately choose to darken the light. John shows Jesus rejecting the framework of stunted preconceptions within which His contemporaries tried to enclose and throttle and sterilize the word of God.

We are told in the eighth chapter of John that Jesus' listeners not only refuse to believe Him, but even call Him mad to justify their unbelief. They bolster their unbelief by a number of unexamined premises, the most obvious of which is the following: *It is unthinkable that God should be sending us a religious figure greater than Abraham.*

This premise has no basis in logic and none in revelation. It was simply another instance of resistance to revelation. It was simply another case of refusing to accept from God truth that man could not verify experimentally. It was hidden adherence to the naturalistic postulate of Protagoras: "Man is the measure of all things."

This naturalistic postulate is the root of atheism. It is never at rest, even in believers. It pretends a *detente* with faith, but its rats' teeth never cease to gnaw away the content of faith and erode its transcendental basis. If it cannot altogether prevent faith, it can at least minimize it.

The believer has always resisted the rats' teeth by counterposing the postulate of faith: *God is the measure of all things.*

The postulate of Protagoras and the postulate of faith are locked in struggle for men's allegiance. When the postulate of faith is in the ascendancy, faith grows strong. When the postulate of naturalism gains the upper hand, faith is slowly throttled.

By the time Jesus came, the Sadducees had eliminated from their faith all belief in angels, spirits and immortality. Their faith was being cut to the measure of unbelief. It was being reduced to a harmless, meaningless residue that could not "interfere" with the "important" aspects of men's lives.

Contemporary parallels can be drawn in our day. The attacks on *Humanae Vitae* sometimes display a total disregard for belief in divine guidance, and rest solely on Protagoras' postulate.

The Sadducees' naturalistic, materialistic principles show up in outcroppings of the Dutch catechism. The commission of cardinals appointed to examine it required that the catechism give adequate treatment of the souls who enjoy the direct vision of God. It also should avoid appearing to say that God can work only those miracles which require no more power than that manifested by nature.

Why do we never win the battle to commit ourselves once and for all to the principle of faith? Jesus gave the answer to the unbelievers in the eighth chapter of John: "Do you know why you can't take in what I say? It is because you are unable to understand My language. The devil is your father, and you prefer to do what your father wants."

It is our preference for ready practicalities over the demands of truth that blind us to truth. It is our hard passions for what we want that blind us to what God wants. It is the violence of man's arrant will set against God's will that drives man to lay hold of Protagoras' postulate as a convenient means of self-justification.

Like most easy answers, this one gives man short shrift in the long run. It may seem to justify man in what he does, but will it help him in the end to get what he really wants?

Jesus cuts across the endless spiral of futile dialectics to show that man's own answers to man will never give man what he needs, but that God's answer to man will provide man with everything he needs, and is therefore the true answer: "I solemnly assure you, if a man keeps My word he will never see death."

In one sentence Jesus exposes the whole sterile irrelevancy of the Sadducees' platform, and challenges the adequacy of the Pharisees' suffocating concept of gaining life everlasting through good works. Human works, no matter how good, cannot open the way to immortality. Protagoras' postulate had infested the faith of the Pharisees too.

The Pharisees were attached, stubbornly attached, to the saving nature of their own works. That is why they were still being pried loose from this self-saving concept long after their conversion to Christ, as we can see from the letter to the Hebrews.

The author of that letter tells us that it is the sacrificial death of Jesus alone which "cleanses our consciences from dead works." Every work that presumes to *create* man's salvation is a dead work. Every work that depends for its ultimate meaning on the saving work of Jesus is a living work.

The Pharisees were no different from the rest of us. We are all overly attached to man's work for man, and never once for all committed to the necessity of God's work for man.

For nearly 2,000 years Christians have ostensibly believed in the saving role of Christ's death on Calvary, and in the power of the ongoing liturgical representation of the mystery of His victimhood. We believe that Christ's own body and blood become present to us there to extend the saving mystery to us personally through Eucharistic Communion. Yet after all this time Christians keep falling away from this hope and turning to something else for comfort.

The faults which the cardinals' commission found in the Dutch catechism's teaching on the saving role of Jesus are only too indicative of this attrition of faith in Jesus. The commission required that the publication clearly state that we inherit from our protoparents a "true state of sin," that Jesus our Redeemer made acceptable satisfaction for our sins, that the sacrifice of the cross and the Sacrifice of the Mass are the sacrifice in which Jesus offered and offers Himself as the holy victim pleasing to God, and that Jesus is really present in the Eucharist through an actual change in the bread.

God is not jealous of the powers He has munificently bestowed on man. He leaves to us, He charges us with the responsibility for, labor for, culture and civilization. He weighs us down with the responsibility of feeding the hundreds of millions of hungry people suffering because human greed cuts back productivity on the basis of its desire to have production controlled by profit motives rather than by human hunger.

God leaves to us the work of cleansing our polluted waterways and our polluted atmosphere; but He warns us that by sin we have also polluted our moral atmosphere with the products of death, and only Christ can restore life. The shibboleths of science have no power at all here. By creating uneven pockets of plenty, science only reveals the more horribly the extent of human selfishness.

The content of our faith is that the ultimate salvation of man lies only in God and in His Christ. The strength of our faith is not measured, however, by mere adherence to these words. The strength of our faith is measured by the shape of our lives. Do our lives take shape around Christ or around the words of Protagoras? When our lives are shaped by Christ and His sacrifice, we have believed.

13

Suffering

It is profoundly tragic that the boy must die to inherit his manhood. It is poignant beyond measure that the girl must die to give birth to her womanhood. It is even more tragic, however, when the price frightens them off, and they cling to perpetual adolescence.

Suffering is inevitable in human life, and the mature face up to the fact. What is more pathetic than the person who meets with shocked surprise the ordinary visitations of suffering? What is more ridiculous than the Christian who thinks he is doing something astounding for Christ when he accepts the ordinary burdens of life which the atheist takes as a matter of course?

Suffering rolls in upon the shores of human life as surely as waves roll in upon the ocean strands. We are finite beings, and finitude means change, and change means simultaneous augmentation and diminishment, contemporaneous death and resurrection.

This casts light on the bitter-sweetness of adolescence. Adolescence is a time of growth; but since there is no growth without change, and since change involves loss as well as gain, there is no human growth without suffering as well as joy.

So long as the finite person is in process he will suffer. He must die to many good things to come alive to others. His life is a graveyard of happy things, but it is also a road upward to things happier still.

There is no need to founder on the shoals of accumulating diminishments that every human voyager experiences. Those shoals lie behind us in our journey. They can never wreck us unless we reverse course and live in the past.

Ahead lies the future with all its hopes and its new life.

Our labors themselves point up a valuable lesson about suffering. We discover that only God can create effortlessly. As for us, we create from the magma of our own substance. Worthwhile accomplishments deplete our energies and our health.

Many great artists and saints were quickly consumed in the very fire of creation from which they drew forth new sparks to illumine man's way. Many parents have spent themselves in the labor of rearing their families. Many statesmen have exhausted themselves in the service of their country, as many soldiers have died for it.

To the burden of suffering imposed by finitude and finite creativity two other burdens of dying have been added. The first is the burden of dying to sin. The second is the burden of dying to finitude, which is an imprisonment we love too much.

By coming alive to the leprous life of sin, our race died to God and inherited mortality. Christ made us die to sin and come alive in Him through baptism. But neither that dying nor that coming alive is completed yet. We can remain Christ's disciples only by bearing in our bodies the suffering of the struggle to die to sin as He did. Each conquest of temptation is a further dying and rising.

We cannot win the victory over temptation without deliberate penance. The Old Testament tells us that fasting and physical discipline turn us from sin, humble us before God, dispose us for prayer, help us to understand spiritual things, and prepare us for God.

The New Testament opens a whole new dimension of suffering and penance by imposing upon us the mighty task of dying to our finitude and opening ourselves to the very life of God. The Gospel tells us that Christ has taken on man's meaning, but it also tells us that He has given man new meaning. Christ not only helps us fulfill our humanity, He lifts us beyond our humanity and makes us die to it as we know it. "For me," Paul declares, "to live is Christ and to die is gain."

This living to Christ and dying to mortal existence was instituted by our baptism. It progresses through our daily living out of the passion-death-resurrection of Jesus.

If we refuse to recognize the need for this series of deaths in the lower regions of being, we will never understand suffering's role in raising us to higher levels of life. Lacking that understanding, we will hate suffering unconditionally, and never reap its fruits.

Not all suffering is from God, but no suffering can occur unless God decides to permit it. Some suffering is neither willed nor wanted by God, for in itself much suffering is useless and destructive and simply a result of sin. Yet it is certain that God brings good out of all suffering endured by those who love Him.

Suffering, if we try to accept it, makes us genuinely God's children. Acceptance of suffering gives us heroic courage to do God's will, whatever it is. It also gives us a tender compassion for others. And suffering accepted releases a flood of creative energies.

A martyr complex toward suffering is nevertheless wrong. Apart from an appropriate degree of penance, which liberates human energies, the human task pleasing to God is reducing to a minimum unnecessary suffering in our own lives and the lives of others.

Jesus set the example by His work of healing. In His own agony, too, He pleaded with the Father to take away the sufferings He faced. However, His plea was provisional, that is, it was dependent on what the Father knew to be best. How much Jesus' prayer alleviated His sufferings we have no way of knowing. We do know that the sufferings He endured alleviated our own.

We ought to observe that Jesus did not deliberately bring His sufferings upon Himself. Nevertheless, He knowingly proceeded with His work even after He saw so clearly the suffering it would bring upon Him. In this He is model for all of us. Christian penitence is exercised primarily "in persevering faithfulness to the duties of one's state of life, in the acceptance of the difficulties arising from one's work and from human coexistence, in a patient bearing of the trials of earthly life and of the utter insecurity which pervades it" (Apostolic Constitution, *Poenitemini*).

To accept suffering as Jesus did, we need His perspective. We are afraid to face death for fear it will make life meaningless. Jesus made the fear itself meaningless. He revealed that it is only in being emptied of mortal life and filled with resurrection-life that man finds his meaning. Labor in field and factory has far more meaning if it helps men on a journey which terminates not in the grave but in the resurrection.

Jesus is the man who succeeded not despite suffering but through suffering. He wove suffering into service. He made suffering meaningful by enduring it out of love. Now who can miss its meaning? Who could wish for greater meaning?

Even a little child can read the message of suffering on Calvary. "He loved me and delivered Himself up for me." "He was wounded for our transgressions, He was bruised for our iniquities; upon Him was the chastisement that made us whole, and with His stripes we are healed."

Closer to us than Calvary is the resurrection-sacrifice that enshrines suffering as the sign of victory. The double consecration recalls the separation of the body and blood of Jesus. It also brings to our altars the teeming life which is the fructification of His suffering.

Jesus nailed all suffering to the cross. Suffering is a species of human experience headed for extinction. Its worst product is death, and death is marked for death.

To faith and intelligence is given the power to unveil the mystery of suffering. In a sinful world, it is love's passage to victory.

14

Hope

We are "sons of God," yet our plans fail, our flesh grows old, and our hospitals are crammed. We speak of God our Father, and yet at times feel more like orphans of the universe. As the author of Psalm 78 testifies, unbelievers see us and sneer: "Where is their God?"

In the eighth chapter of his letter to the Romans, St. Paul squarely faces this redemptive gap. Our spirits have indeed been lifted to rebirth, but our flesh continues to go down to death. Thought of this makes us give vent to groans of anguish over hope delayed. Paul shores up our courage by reminding us that present sufferings are as nothing compared with the glory we are to become. We can only wait in faith for the time when God will do what He alone can do — redeem our bodies so that we may "never sleep in death."

These considerations involve us in eschatological meditation, that is, in meditation that resonates with longing for more than earth can offer, more than nature can give, more than man can accomplish.

Paul helps us to see and feel the struggle in man and all nature to give birth to something beyond their powers. The project begins to come into focus, and we begin to see clearly that the realization of our hope depends on God. Without man's cooperation, our hope will not be fulfilled; without God's, it cannot be fulfilled.

Our objective includes resurrection from the dead, and this demands God's personal involvement. To forget this is tragic and irrational. The blunder of the Chosen People was to let this fact go out of focus. Their mistake was to take too much on their own shoulders, and leave too little to God.

The result was failure. In trying to do more than they could, they failed to do even what they could. They did not keep the Law. This is Paul's explicit teaching, found in the ninth chapter of the letter to the Romans.

"Israel, looking for a righteousness derived from law," Paul wrote, "failed to do what the law required. Why did they fail? Because they relied on good deeds instead of trusting in faith."

We must reflect on this mistake because history tends to repeat itself, and we have moved into an era of activism and Christian responsibility which is wide open to the activist error of the Jews which both Jesus and St. Paul condemned.

The Achilles' heel of human thought is its tendency to extremism. The last place the pendulum of human ideas ever stops is the middle, which is the only position of balance! The extremism of simplistic ideas seems much more satisfying to finite minds than a synthesis of ideas, where truth generally lies.

We either want God to do all, or we want to do all. Cooperation is the most difficult. The result is that some of those Christians who have been awakened to the work they must do are downgrading the importance of the sacramental mysteries. They are esteeming their efforts over their adoration. They are tempted to find time more important than eternity, and man's work more important than God's. They are tempted to call the social works of the Church more important than the divine workings within the Church.

All this calls to mind the imprecations of Jesus upon the blind guides of old: "You say, 'If anyone swears by the altar, it is nothing; but if anyone swears by the gift that is on the altar, he is bound by his oath.' You blind men! For which is greater, the gift or the altar that makes the gift sacred?"

There is an event in the beginning of the fifth chapter of Luke which can set our thinking straight once more. Jesus commandeers

Peter's boat, and teaches from it, and all listen. We must listen to Jesus where He speaks, or we will not hear Him. He speaks from the Church He founded on Peter. We must do what we hear, or our listening is useless.

Jesus commands Peter to fish, and Peter fishes, though his night's fishing had been futile. His fishing at Jesus' command produces a superabundance. Jesus tells what it means: "I will make you fishers of men."

The radiance of this miracle dims the importance of all human activity by comparison. Jesus worked the work of God, and the young men were staggered by the wonder of it. When they recovered themselves, they were no longer living in the old world where man depends primarily on himself and his possessions. They rose up, "left everything and followed Him."

One of the most dismal errors issuing from the newly self-inflated importance of certain groups of Christians is their belittling of the evangelical life lived according to poverty, chastity, and obedience, in the likeness of the Apostles and of Jesus Himself.

Jesus founded the evangelical life of the counsels for His own sake, and for the preaching of the Gospel. Nothing is more becoming than that some young men and women should renounce the most attractive ways of ordinary human life to follow the divine Christ. And nothing is more effective than to have men and women called by God to live out before the eyes of the people of God the grandeur and the rigor of the Sermon on the Mount.

The Church needs this witness, because while all are not called to the religious life, all are called to live its spirit. Every Christian must be ready to give up what the religious has actually given up, rather than betray Christ, when trial comes.

The religious life is impervious to the fluctuations of human evaluations, for its value was set by Christ. "If you would be perfect . . . follow Me." It is the life Jesus lived and invited others to live — in fact if they are called to it, and in spirit if they are not.

It is the most perfect expression of a son's love for God. Through living it Himself, Jesus revealed Trinitarian love to us. We learn what Trinitarian love is by this poor, virginal and obedient life of Jesus. Better than anything else, it shows that our hope for the future is in God.

15

Love

Many heads believe "God is Love," but few hearts understand what that means.

God's Love is the Person who, in the beginning, hovered over *tohu wa-bohu,* the black pit of nothingness. In the beginning He hovered there, divine Love and Eros, who sent the fiery nebulas spinning through the abyss in the galactic spirals of His breath.

It is on His account the stars do not staidly shine, but twinkle across the iridescences from incarnadine to amethyst. He it is who sends the fireflies, those living lanterns, drifting through dark night's warm air shining with love until mate discovers mate.

It was this Love's breath of tenderness in the clay that brought life: "In the image of God He created him; male and female He created them." It is His doing that makes mate seek mate, and travel together up the heavens and down the limbos of wedded love, and in oneness become quickeners of the new life springing from their holy passion to know in its turn the mystery of love.

Love overshadowed the Virgin "and the Word was made flesh and dwelt among us." With unutterable groanings the Love groaned in Jesus, who lived for us and pitched His tent with us. "I have longed and longed to eat . . . with you. . . ." He ate and drank with us, then suffered and died and rose for us as the Love drove Him.

Love made us into Him with the water and the fire. "They shall be no longer two but one. . . ." The tongues on Pentecost were "as flames" — the real flames were kindled not in the tongues seen but in the hearts within. The burning hearts drove the disciples of Jesus to far lands while the fire within spread to their tongues and they spoke with flames the world neither would nor could extinguish.

This is the fire that made the world and now sets it aflame, not to destroy it but to consummate it. In it one melts only in the arms of another, and its burning anoints with the dew of joy.

It is the fire that burns down every wall and fuses everything without destroying anything. It burns down even the barriers between heaven and earth, God and man: "If anyone loves Me he will keep My word. Then My Father will love him and we shall come to him and make our dwelling place with him."

The Fire that descends since Pentecost is Fire from the Heart of the Son. It burns away rebellious wills and implants new hearts, with the supple warmth of sonliness, as Jeremiah foretold.

This divine Fire sets our hearts aflame not with any kind of fire, but above all with the flame of filial love for the Father in the likeness of Jesus who said: "The world must be brought to know that I love the Father and that I am doing exactly what the Father told Me." This Fire ignites the universe in fulfillment of the will of Jesus who said: "And would that it were already enkindled!"

On the day of Pentecost when the disciples poured from the house full of the Spirit, even the foreigners heard them speaking in their own languages. *The native tongue of every man is love.* All are not practiced in speaking it, but all understand it easily when it is spoken.

Jesus sends us His Holy Spirit, the third Person of the Blessed Trinity, as His gift of Love. This Love helps us to discriminate between all good and evil influences and courses of action.

The Love of Jesus is not the love of justice that promotes justice by violence; nor is it the love of unity that compels unity by force; nor the love of truth that bolsters one's own convictions by forcing other men to mouth them. These self-loves do not dismantle walls; they only rearrange them to make new prisons.

The Love of Jesus teaches us the way of Jesus: "The Paraclete, the Holy Spirit . . . will teach you everything and remind you of all that I have told you." This Spirit promotes justice by teaching us to surpass justice by giving beyond anyone's due. It promotes truth by teaching us we are free and responsible for arriving at our own convictions, and for making our own decisions; but this Spirit of Sonliness teaches us unflagging sonly obedience to God and all legitimate authority in matters of both truth and action.

Pentecost located the new Sinai and the new Sion. By the old covenant of Sinai and the life in the old Sion men were committed to renouncing the loveless disobedience of Adam and Eve. By the events of Pentecost the storm and the fire that signalled God's presence on Sinai have moved and located themselves upon us. The Christian assembly is the new Sinai and the new Sion where God resides.

The vial of Sonship was broken open on the cross to suffuse Christ's members with His Sonly Spirit. Pentecost was the day His members carried His Spirit forth to suffuse the whole world. It is the day of the dissemination of the Church.

On Pentecost there was a hurricane sound of violence, but no one was injured. There were flaming tongues of fire but no one was scorched. The mighty cataract of this Love is so holy it sweeps passions' powers to their peak and yet averts disaster. Inebriation is deepest and love most ascendant forever now, for those who drink of the cup of the love of God.

16

Gratitude

Anyone who tries to lift himself by his own bootstraps is no suitable candidate for a doctorate in physics. He might in fact lack much more than a knowledge of science.

In the third chapter of his letter to the Galatians we find St. Paul exposing the equally foolish "Operation *Spiritual* Bootstrap." The rationale of Operation Spiritual Bootstrap is the belief that our own works are powerful enough to save us. Men always like to think they are self-sufficient. Human pride always listens to the words: "You will be as gods."

Paul explains that the Old Law was not given to the Jews so that by keeping it they might save themselves. It was given to them to teach them Operation Bootstrap works no better against the force of evil than it does against the force of gravity.

The Law was actually given to the Jews to teach them by experience that they could not save themselves by being good precisely because men are incapable of being good by themselves. The Law taught them how sinful they were and how much they needed God's salvation. It prepared them for Jesus.

How angry Paul would be to see the same tired old heresy of do-it-yourself salvation being trotted out today for consumption by the gullible! Today's version begins by fudging over belief in the revealed doctrine of original sin. In the process it denies the existence of Adam and Eve, whom God and the teaching Church affirm. (See Pope Paul's "Credo of the People of God.") Finally it sees in Christ only a good man who did not redeem us but merely set a good example which we can and must follow by a do-it-yourself operation.

Actually Christ was sent to us to put an end to the irrational Operation Spiritual Bootstrap. Man cannot forgive sin. God alone can. Man cannot give himself immortality. God can and will, in Christ.

By putting us under the dispensation of faith Christ Himself has lifted us up to a new order of holiness and power for good deeds. This is the point Paul makes.

In the seventeenth chapter of St. Luke we have an example of what our response should be. Ten lepers were healed by Jesus, but only one had the goodness to come back and express his gratitude.

Similarly, faith has freed us from Operation Spiritual Bootstrap, but it has not freed us from the obligation of being good. It has really deepened the obligation of being good because through Christ we have the strength to fulfill the obligation to goodness.

As Paul indicates to the Galatians, we cannot first cause holiness by being good; rather we can be good only after God has made us holy in Christ. We cannot be rivers of goodness until we are joined to the sea that is Christ.

The obligation of being good was not met by nine out of ten cured lepers. Is it being met by us? Traditional sexual morality is being attacked today in the name of St. Paul. The "new morality" capitalizes on St. Paul's teaching about freedom, but hedges on his insistence that there are objective norms of goodness and sexual purity.

What can we say about the "new morality" in such areas as sex? Has Christ's new law of love annulled our obligation to avoid adultery and fornication?

I will answer by another question: has God annulled our human nature or only perfected it? Clearly, He has not annulled it but has made it perfect in Jesus. Then He has not annulled the obligations that inseparably accompany it. As long as we are finite creatures with physical bodies, there are some things which accord with our nature and are good, and others which harm it and are bad.

As long as we have human nature in its earthly state there are things which we are responsible for doing, and things we cannot responsibly do. The natural law is still making its demands, and Jesus and Paul and the teaching Church all insist on our fulfilling them.

In a milder way than the Jewish Law, the natural law serves as a constant reminder of our sinfulness and our continuing need for our Savior. Pope Paul adverted to this in his encyclical on the holy use of sex in marriage.

Speaking of those who are struggling but failing to avoid sins against their marriage, Pope Paul wrote: "And if sin should keep its hold over them, let them not be discouraged, but rather have recourse with humble perseverance to the mercy of God, which is poured forth in the sacrament of penance. In this way they will be enabled to achieve the fullness of conjugal life. . . ."

Christ provided us with the sacrament of penance to free us from the leprosy of sin committed after baptism. Those who ignore this sacrament or complain about it or simply refuse to use it have one thing in common with the nine lepers: they share ingratitude.

17
Joy

Who can take hold of that fleeting phantom *Joy* in the hour when it comes laughing into our lives, and scientifically analyze its components, and say: "This is *true* joy"?

We have seen and experienced those glorious moments, but no one has ever distilled their essence or captured their secret. A man in the flush of victory, a girl on her wedding day, a woman on the day of motherhood — all drink at the same fountain of inebriation, but each would tell of joy in a different way.

Whatever the secret of joy, Jesus invites us to the secret of how to possess it. "Ask and you shall receive," Jesus says, "that your joy may be complete." This joy from Jesus is not the world's fading flower of a moment. It is true joy. It is a reality far beyond words which invites us to profound reflection.

Joy is a gift from God, but it is also the distillation of our fidelity and the radiance of our love. Jesus explained this at the Last Supper. "If you keep My commandments you will remain in My love," He promised, and added, "I have told you this so that My joy may be in you and your joy may be complete."

Joy is God's gift; it is also the effluvium of our faithful love; and it is our delight in freedom.

St. James speaks in his letter about the "law of freedom" under which Christians live. We like to say we are "under law" or "at liberty." What then is the "law of freedom"? Why is it not rather freedom without law?

The answer lies in the fact that human nature cannot escape the limitations of its finitude or the responsibilities of its obligations, but it does have the freedom to love and accept rather than hate and reject itself as it is. It can choose to rejoice in the really human activities it has the power to perform, and abhor all the actions it can undertake which in the end would destroy self and community.

Man can love and act rightly but it is difficult, and the difficulty is expressed by the *law of connaturality*. The *law of connaturality* tells us that we act with ease and pleasure only when we act according to our natural state. Our natural state is that of good creatures partly corrupted by a long history of sin.

This taint of inner corruption made it impossible for historical man to be wholly good and wholly human without constantly resisting certain connatural actions. In the ordinary course of events, then, the man who wanted to be most fully human had to follow a law given him from outside. This exteriority of the law made law as if it were man's master, and man became not master but slave of the law of goodness. Such was the state of affairs under the Old Law.

The freedom to love and live the fully good human life belongs only to the man who observes, not a law outside himself, but a law identified with himself. Just as evil men enjoy doing evil because they are following the inner law of their own corruption, the good man can love fully human goodness only when the law of total goodness is written into his inner nature.

This law of total goodness is written into a man's nature at baptism. We gain some insight into how this can come about by observing how man himself modifies natures. The nature of metal is to fall when released in air, yet by spreading the metal into wings and changing the air to jets, man makes metal fly.

It is precisely in such a context of human transformation that St. James writes his words about the "law of freedom." God, James tells us, has seeded our hearts with His word, and has made us "the first specimens of His new creation." We who have been baptized into a rebirth of nature have thereby become citizens of the law of freedom.

Fidelity to our new law of freedom introduces us to true joy. Joy is psychic pleasure that accompanies our noble free acts. Joy is the climate of good men who love rightly and possess what they love — God and truth and lives attuned to both.

The true joy which the children of God possess is not anchored in themselves or their possessions. Even should crops fail and barns be empty, Habakkuk proclaims, "I will rejoice in the Lord and exult in my saving God."

The joyous wisdom of the dedicated Christian works for the good of others, but does not depend on their gratitude. It abounds in good health, but it does not depend on health. It can even superabound in suffering, providing suffering be the result of fidelity to Christ.

It is true that men and events can wound our joy. Even the *Man of Joy* was thrown to His knees by men and made the *Man of Sorrows*. We too will have suffering in the world, Jesus tells us; at the same time He consoles us by saying, "But be brave; I have overcome the world."

Events can momentarily eclipse our joy, but nothing can destroy it, for its source hovers high above the reach of this world's clouds and storms. The source of Christian joy is faith. Faith is anchored in the most high God. Out of faith streams hope in God's promises, and love of Him — and love's corona is joy.

The greatest Christian invitation to joy is the Mass. The Mass is our most intense enactment of faith, our momentary transcending of hope, our transitory possession of God-made-risen-flesh. There, wise parents (who by their own power can give their children the bread of tears) introduce their offspring to the Bread of Joy. The coruscations of the Eucharistic event bathe the whole world in a promising moment of God's love. And that is joy:

For thy sweet love remember'd such wealth brings
That then I scorn to change my state with kings.

18

Self-Esteem

The young girl grew tired of recounting her dreams to the psychiatrist, so she summarized the lot of them: "They all come to the same thing. I'm always somebody important!"

We all need that sense of self-esteem the girl was trying to build up, and we have a right to cultivate it. What we do not have is a right to escalate our own importance at the cost of someone else's.

The people who do that have God's judgment expressed for them in the parable of the Pharisee and the tax collector. The self-important Pharisee leaves Church without God's friendship; the man with the sense of sin walks home with God.

If the parable of the Pharisee and the tax collector warns us against pride, Paul's first letter to the Corinthians tells us how to develop humility. The letter was addressed to the Corinthians at a time when they were disintegrating into factions. Some prided themselves on being Peter's converts; others, Paul's; others, Apollos'.

"Is Christ divided?" Paul demands to know. "Was Paul crucified for you? Or were you baptized in the name of Paul?" Thus Paul tramples mercilessly on the folly of men so easily diverted from Christ to theologism and personality cults.

While engaged in this decimation of empty honors, Paul takes up the matter of spiritual gifts or charisms. There are different gifts, ministries and functions, Paul admits, but only one Spirit who gives them, only one Lord whom they serve, only one God toward whom they are directed. There is only one body of Christ to which these various gifts belong, and which they are destined to serve.

No matter what our gifts, we have no basis for the folly of pride. None of us can say, "I am my own." We belong to Christ as a man's members belong to himself. We belong to one another as the various parts of a body mutually support the one life they share.

It is tragic divisiveness to carry on a family feud as to which member is more important. What is really important in the body of Christ is that each member execute the function which is the one he is best equipped to perform. We are finite and limited beings who can be effective and happy only by making the best use of the powers we actually have.

It is a yet worse evil when we neglect our role in the hierarchical structure of the Church to interfere in someone else's. What I refer to is not consultation but usurpation. There are priests who want to tell the bishops what to do, and laymen who want to tell both. What I refer to are not suggestions and proposals, which are in order, but demands, which are not.

Such demands are reared on the foundation of jealousy which feeds on overesteem of the ecclesial function of another. Paul explodes this foundation by reducing to rubble our false evaluations of the various roles in the Church. God, he says, has given greater honor to inferior parts of the body so as to avoid wrangling. One thinks of comely features, which are so praised, yet are far less important to life than many other body functions.

Many members are jealous of authority, which is important to the body of Christ, yet is in itself far less a gift to the person exercising it than many other charisms. To control a city is nothing if the man who controls it lacks self-control.

Power is esteemed in every realm, and the lion is an admired beast; but who has ever shown that God loves the lion more than the lamb? In C.S. Lewis' Narnia allegories, Christ is a lion, but He is a very different kind of lion who has many friends and is a danger to none of them, but only to His enemies. This is consonant with

Scripture, but Scripture prefers to identify Christ with the lamb.

Christ is identified as a lamb to deflate the blowfish of pride in all of us. We ought to remember, however, that we cannot deflate it by either sincere or pretended underestimation of the self. Consciously or subconsciously we react to such a lie. Humility is the truth, but it is the truth not only about ourselves, but about the whole mosaic of human living of which we are but one unit. Humility is not depreciation of the self but appreciation of others.

Belittling what we have is wrong. Realizing we don't have everything is right. And so Paul urges us to learn to "live according to the Scripture, that none of you may be puffed up in favor of one against another."

Just as self-depreciation is a false road to humility, so too is it wrong to withhold praise of others. Due praise withheld is not a source of humility but of pride. It tempts the one unpraised to despise the judgments of others, and this is the road to arrogance. Praise given in due measure helps a man establish that genuine, solid self-esteem which is resistant to both pride and despair. Furthermore, it helps us to dare difficult but worthwhile things. That is why, in this very letter on moderation, Paul praises so highly the state of virginal commitment to Christ which is of such great service to God and Church.

Paul never ends on a negative note. He not only urges us to moderate our sense of competition by the spirit of brotherly unity, he also tells us where we can give our competitive urge an exhausting workout to the benefit of all.

"I will show you a more excellent way," Paul says, and launches into his encomium to love, leaving the charisms growing small beneath. "Make love your aim," he urges. Aspiring to love undermines all contention and promotes all service. For "love is not jealous or boastful; it is not arrogant or rude. Love does not insist on its own way. . . . Love never ends."

19

The Meaning of Mary

So profound is Mary in being and meaning that every depiction of her is a distortion of her. Stress on her transcendent privileges conjures up a false gap between her and us. Stress on her common lot with us falsely deprecates her unmatched glory.

If we seek Mary in herself we will never find her. If we seek her as simply one of us we will never know her. Mary can be discovered only in combination with God and us.

What happens to Mary in Scripture is clearly beyond the ordinary. What Mary herself does is hardly extraordinary. Revelation bursts from this conjunction. *By being extraordinary in what she receives and ordinary in what she does, Mary reveals both the meaning of Christ and the meaning of man.*

Mary was an unpretentious girl. She was surprised and afraid when specially praised. She mothered her son, and resided with Him for thirty years in the quiet shadows of ordinary life. She lived on the outer edges of His public life, suffered at His death, and is last found praying with His followers after His resurrection.

This is what she did, but Scripture also tells what was done for her, and the two together are undoubtedly the roots of the rising symphony of praise to Mary that has mounted with the centuries.

A solid examination of Mary's prerogatives makes us embrace Mary as one of us, and makes us glad to honor her as one lifted beyond us. Mary is always only the creature, but she is always with God. Among creatures there is none who matches her as the purest revelation of religion.

Mary is the virginal mother of Divinity. This is what she is and what she means. All else disposes for this or flows from it.

Mary's motherhood serves first of all as revelation. It reveals not her but God. It is the passive side of divine action. In His comings and goings in history, God initiates. In His relations with creation, He comes with majestic at-homeness, He fecundates superabundantly, and He leaves the fecundated ones more virginal than before, yet wedded to Him.

From creation's side of the interchange comes Mary's "Be it done to me." Mary's "Yes" is the purest symbol of creation's role. All creation, in every interchange with God, shares the feminine role of loving submission. This is verified in the life of Jesus. His "Yes" to God is even more of a submission than Mary's. It is maintained within a bloody sweat and an insanity of torture.

Yet the woman will always remain the better symbol of the submissive love all who love must give to God. The very fact that Jesus also had to receive the submission of others obscures His own. Mary's is never obscured.

Mary's "Yes" is the morning star "Yes" to God that pre-announced the full day of Jesus' own eternal "Yes." *Every creature must accept their "Yes" and make it his own if he expects to keep his life always or to give it to others in its eternal character.*

That is why Vatican II's Constitution on the Church tells all who work in the apostolate that they must be fittingly animated by a maternal love like Mary's.

Mary's Immaculate Conception was God's betrothal gift to His virginal bride-mother. Mary's immaculateness is the sweet beckoning call to the Creator to come and enter and make everything live.

Mary's immaculateness serves us all. Primal innocence, product of the Creator alone, is an incomparable hierophany. It makes of Mary not only God's door to man, but man's window to God.

We must share Mary's immaculateness, not merely honor it.

By no other way can we ever see God. We began sharing in it through the tardy immaculate conception of our baptism.

Mary's immaculateness also means that she is the new Eve reversing the first Eve's refusal to say "Yes." She is the new creation, harbinger of a new earth and a new heaven. Her own assumption immortal into heaven was already contained in promise in her Immaculate Conception.

Mary's Immaculate Conception is God's promise to us. She received it "by foreseen merits of the death of Christ." What she received by anticipation we can receive in due time by the Son she has given us.

Mary's primary intercession for us was her "Yes" by which she became ontological mediator, not between us and Christ, but by giving us Christ. Mary herself is only the firstfruit of Christ's work. She is the one of us most perfectly redeemed by Him. Only by His grace is she a channel of His grace. The Constitution on the Church accordingly tells us that her titles "are to be so understood that they neither take away from or add anything to the dignity and efficacy of Christ the one Mediator."

True devotion to Mary lies in knowing her true excellence, loving her for it, and daring to become her offspring — that is, imitating her until we become in a belated way what she was from the beginning.

Is the current wane of devotion to Mary a reality or only an illusion? Is it fault or development? The fuller the presence of Jesus, the fainter by comparison appears Mary the Morning Star. Is today's seeming decline occasioned by our remissness, or by the light of the approach of the Second Coming?

In any case, the yearly feast of the Immaculate Conception is each time the rising of the Morning Star. When Mary comes, day cannot be far behind. Where Mary is, Christ is never far away. Mary the Immaculate Conception is she who promises Christ:

His only Son He sent to exile
In the Egypt of the womb
Till Mary as a fountain brought Him forth
A torrent of Love bringing floodtime
To the delta
Of the world.

PART THREE

20

Revelation

Shalom ("peace") was Jesus' greeting to His Apostles on the day of His resurrection. Jesus' salutation of peace is not to be confused with the wishful thinking of the worldly. Jesus was not *wishing* His followers peace. He was *giving* it to them in power that evening. "Shalom," He repeated; and then He breathed forth on them the same Spirit that hovered over the abyss during the eons of creation. Concomitantly with Jesus' breath, His Spirit went forth anew to create the world of reconciliation with God.

"Receive the Holy Spirit," Jesus continued. "If you forgive men's sins, they are forgiven; if you hold them, they are held fast." The peace between man and God that was annihilated by sin has been resurrected by the innocence of Christ.

"Whatever is begotten by God overcomes the world," John tells us in his first letter. Christ, begotten of God, overcame the world and offered it peace. In us, our faith is begotten of God, and therefore by it we conquer the world and share Christ's peace and joy.

Thomas shared neither joy nor peace on the day of Jesus' resurrection, for he lost a battle to unbelief. God spoke to Thomas through the witness of the other Apostles: "We have seen the

Lord!" Thomas refused God's witness there. He demanded that God speak to Him directly through Jesus. Thomas chose darkness to the humiliation of receiving God's message through his equals.

We choose light. We are a wall of light projected across 2,000 years along which the message of life is passed. We are a Niagara of faith, coursing down the centuries, destined to rush to fulfillment in the triumph of the resurrection.

Neither is all well, however, with us. There are eddies and backwaters along the course where many are caught in the stagnation of unbelief. The eternal recurrent need to accept a middleman in faith is repeatedly rejected.

In the very manner of contemporary response to Christ's offer of peace, trouble is brewing. Men want to remember the part about God forgetting our sins and forget the part about God remembering our sins. Picking and choosing their revelation as Thomas did that morning, they want the peace of God's forgiveness through His Church without the purgation of confession to His Church. They want the deep infection cleaned out without the pain of cauterizing the wound.

Oblivious to the lesson of Thomas, various Christian schools are toying with two other dangerous delusions. The first is the facile belief that the hierarchy can arrive at the truth in all things without consulting the laity. The second delusion is that the body of Christians can be faithful to Christ without the authentic role of Pope and bishops in matters of faith and morals.

From the time of the Apostle-bishop Thomas, there has been the tradition in the Church that, before they speak, bishops must listen to the brethren. Not only did Thomas receive witness from the other Apostles; not only did Peter, Prince of the Apostles, receive and accept correction from Paul; but Christ commissioned a woman to carry first news of the resurrection to the Apostolic College. Mary Magdalene proudly bears the title: "Apostle to the Apostles." The tradition has continued in such women as St. Catherine of Siena, who counselled Popes.

The healthy movement for more consultation of the laity is simply an expression of the fact that, in serious affairs, the whole Church gathers together to reflect on her problems and God's answers. The purpose is not to count heads but to hear all in order to find truth wherever it is. The precedents mentioned above warn us not to set up grades and rubrics against truth.

The Spirit speaks where He will, and we must listen where He speaks. The conclusion, however, is obviously *not* that truth is arrived at by counting hands.

That is the second dangerous current delusion, that truth is the product of Gallup poles. *What people want and what they do can be polled, but not what they ought to want and ought to do.* Even in secular courts, the jury does not count the number of witnesses to make its decision; it is ready to count one witness for more than all the rest together if the one seems to be the only one with the facts. Similarly, in the Church, everyone is free to speak, not that we may count hands, but that we may sift truth.

A companion delusion is the notion that theologians are the spokesmen of the Church. Except for an arrogant theologian here or there, this is a mistake not of theologians but of their adherents.

The work of theologians, like the opinion of the body of Christians, is subject to the final judgment of the court of truth appointed for the Church by Christ Himself. That court, which is made up of Pope and bishops under the direct guidance of the Holy Spirit, is the authentic guiding and teaching body in the Church. It is called the magisterium, and it is responsible for guiding the whole Church along the way of the one faith. Without it the Christian body disintegrates into sects which can hardly be called one in Christ. Of these chosen guides Christ said: "He who hears you hears Me."

Fortunately for Thomas, Jesus gave him the personal revelation he demanded. But Jesus blessed not him but us: "You have believed because you have seen Me. Happy those who have not seen but have believed."

In our own way, though, we too are graced with personal experience of Jesus. Jesus manifests Himself to each of us personally in the mystery of the Church. The heart of the Church is our assembly around the Eucharistic Christ. There we are made one in Jesus and in His Holy Spirit.

St. John, whose teaching is intensely sacramental and Eucharistic, turns our faith to the sacramental mysteries in his first letter. He tells us there that Jesus came to men in the reality of blood and water and His testifying Spirit. The blood and the water refer to the outpouring from the side of Jesus on Calvary. The Church from the beginning has recognized that event as sacramental in nature. It was Jesus' death which gives us life through the water of baptism and the blood of the Eucharist. The truth of this is witnessed to by the Holy Spirit whom Jesus sent forth to us when He bowed His head and died.

John is telling us that the People of God assemble around the Eucharist not simply to recall what happened to the Apostles, but to share in the happening. Jesus is genuinely present to us and active for us in His mysteries, and His Spirit is actually testifying within us, confirming our faith.

One can wonder whether the other Apostles failed in some way to be the sign to Thomas which would have shored up his tottering belief. Certainly Thomas, who was invited to put his hand into the open wound in the side of Jesus, remains a great pillar of our own faith. He went forth to be a great sign of Christ to the world.

We should be witnesses strengthened in our own way by our Eucharistic meetings with Jesus. We project the power and goodness of Christ into the world. We are or ought to be the *locus* from which God addresses the world around us.

21

Change in the Church

At first the Good News of Jesus trickled out of Palestine in insignificant freshets. With the centuries the waves of its strength mounted, sweeping away those civilizations which staked their existence on ability to stamp out this late florescence of man's inner life and freedom.

Jesus' parable of the mustard seed and parable of the yeast stand witness to the foretelling of the miraculous mystery of phenomenal growth this kingdom of heaven would have on earth. The mustard seed parable best foretells the kingdom's self-contained growth, and the yeast parable its effect on all men.

The coupling of these two parables is sometimes accredited, not to Jesus, but to Matthew, for the reason that Mark shows a different coupling. He joins the mustard seed parable with that of the seed growing secretly.

With experience of itinerant preaching like Jesus' own, I propose another explanation. Jesus taught for several years, so that He must have repeated most parables many times with many variations. It is likely, therefore, that Jesus originated both couplings, on different occasions, under different circumstances. It would have been on some occasion when both men and women were present that Jesus directed the seed parable to the farmers and the yeast parable to the housewives.

Jesus thereby gave a new turn to the revelation. The parable of the yeast adds two emphases of striking significance today.

Compare the seed's action with the yeast's. Plant the tiny, barely visible mustard seed beside Lake Galilee where Jesus taught and where the mustard plants grew, and within the year it will spring up into a flowering herb taller than a man. That is rapid growth.

Knead yeast into dough, however, and in no time the tiny additive will cause the whole mass to stir in ferment. This phenomenon is characteristic of the transforming stir Christianity has brought to earth since the time of Jesus.

The ferment seizes both the Church-kingdom's members, and those outside. The ferment is the sign of growth and the upheaval of onrushing life meeting resistance.

Growth is change not only in size but in characteristics. The marvel of the single fertilized cell that grows into the mustard seed and then the herb lies not only in its power of mitosis but in its power of cell differentiation. The cells not only subdivide to increase the size of the organism, but they specialize to produce its complexity. One becomes root, another branch, another leaf or flower or fruit.

The Church, too, continues to grow in complexity as well as in size. Those who fear all change in the Church ought to reflect that the Church must undergo change like the growing mustard seed. It too must grow, develop, differentiate, flower and fructify.

Those who fear no change whatsoever ought to remember that the Church's growth and change must follow the laws of differentiation which apply to every living organism. The organism which does not grow in fidelity to its own genetics grows cancerous or monstrous. In either case it ends up in ontological self-alienation. *It is no more.*

Interestingly enough, the parable of the yeast contains the germ of this truth. Yeast is a living organism *which produces change in other bodies while itself remaining unchanged.* The Christian must externalize his inner Christ-life for the benefit of all men and live in harmony with them, yet not permit his interaction with secularism to infect and malform his own Christian interior. God's Spirit is the sole life of Christians.

The two parables end with a quote from Psalm 78: "I will open my mouth in parables, I will announce what has lain hidden since creation." The Psalm makes it clear that not only the author will do this, but that his listeners and fellow believers must do it. He passes on to them their forefathers' memories of God's mighty works and self-revelation, and they in turn must pass on in uncorrupted word and example that same message.

We are the parable of Christ, we are the salt of the earth, we are the unadulterated yeast in the dough of mankind. Not that in bad faith we already pretend we are perfect. Rather we have reason to remember and make our own the words of tenth-century King Alfred of England, who wrote: "The name alone we loved, that we were Christians, and very few of the virtues."

That is why we are so aware of the need for change in the Church. We must change and grow more like Christ. We must continue to remember that we are the Pilgrim Church in trek to God, yet we can never forget that we are the Servant Church involved in movement toward man. The terminus of the Church is not only divinization, but humanization.

The kingdom comes "unawares" and is "within," Jesus said. Not that He was demanding divorce from creation or creativity or the world of men. He was, though, mandating concentration on the inner renewal that will be the yeast of a world in transformation.

He *was* forbidding identification with the inner world of those men who reject the inner world of the kingdom. He was turning our hearts to love of the Bread which nourishes the inner man, and training us to "await the coming down from heaven of God's Son whom He raised from the dead, Jesus. . . ."

If Christian in more than name, we do await that moment of our maturity. The yeast will have done its work then, and we can enjoy the feast.

22

New Doctrines

Most theologians cherish their doctor of divinity degree, but not Mr. Fiddle, who refused his. "It's bad enough being Fiddle," he explained, "without being Fiddle D.D."

Theologians come to our attention nowadays because Jesus warned us against false prophets, and the theologians are doing most of the prophesying in today's Church. "By their fruits" we must separate the good theologians from the bad ones.

Mankind is masterminding a changed age. The Church guides the man of faith into this new age. It teaches him to adjust gladly to what he can, but to hold firmly to what he must. The dinosaurs are not our exemplars. They failed to adjust to the changing earth. To find them now, you get a shovel or visit a museum. Christ the ever-new is our exemplar.

In response to the call for renewal, many prophetic voices rise in the Church. To which shall we listen? How tell the good fruit from the poison? Both Scripture and tradition give us the guidelines for judgment.

"All I command you, you must keep and observe, adding nothing to it, taking nothing away," God says in Deuteronomy. "If a prophet or dreamer of dreams arises among you and offers to do a sign or a wonder for you, and the sign or wonder comes about, and if he then says to you, 'Come, then, let us follow other gods. . . ,' you are not to listen. . . ."

The guideline here is that the new must not contradict what we have already received. "A disciple is not above his teacher," Jesus points out. *The rule is that a prophet must explain Christ, not change Him or His teaching.* Whoever changes Christ's teaching sets himself above Christ. He is a false prophet. In good English, he is a fraud.

John's first letter warns us: "Beloved, do not believe every spirit; test the spirits to see whether they are of God." His second letter adds: "There are many deceivers about in the world, refusing to admit that Jesus Christ has come in the flesh. They are the Deceiver; they are the Antichrist. Watch yourselves, or all our work will be lost and not get the reward it deserves. If anyone does not keep within the teaching of Christ but goes beyond it, he cannot have God with him. . . ."

"If anyone comes to you bringing a different doctrine," John writes, "you must not receive him in your house or even give him a greeting."

The Church's call for renewal is being obstructed by the sluggards and the cowards who disobey the call under the guise of faith. They are by no means to be exonerated, but we are concerned here with the false prophets who subvert the renewal by false doctrine.

The false prophets are those caravans of dissident Catholics who obstinately set out in new directions apart from the Church and contrary to her doctrine and commands. They distort the whole nature of revealed religion by failing to make the radical distinction between deism and theism.

The deist is one who comes to a knowledge of God the Creator solely by observing and thinking about the cosmos. Deism blossoms in every age. It holds that God created the world, but left to us the discovery of life's meaning and the laws of right conduct. Our sole guide is reason well used.

The theist believes his religion is rooted in history. He believes that God revealed Himself by entering into history and remaining at work in history, in fellowship with man.

Theism differs from deism through having a fixed historical

content which cannot be changed any more than the history of Rome can be changed. We can ignore, distort, or falsify Roman history, but we cannot change it. No more can we change what Jesus did and said.

To falsify the history of God's doings and demands in the interest of renewal is to prune the tree by cutting its roots. It would seem that no one would commit such folly, but to ignore tradition and the ecclesial authority which safeguard it is to commit such folly. It cuts the lifeline of history by which we breathe in Christ. It gives birth to a cancerous "Christian" deism which mushrooms without the roots of historical revelation.

Christians who ignore tradition are fashioning dissident centers of cosmic architecture. They are trying to close the door of history in the face of God. Their action is of the very essence of sin, which is to play god with God's law. "You will be like gods," is the first and the greatest temptation.

The fruit of the false prophet is tainted by the poisons of novelty, arrogance and obstinacy. He is not a son who, like Jesus, does only what He sees His Father do. In most cases, too, he teaches an easy morality under the guise of love.

Yet the truth is that life is a warfare and nothing is more demanding than love. How we must struggle to be faithful to our love! Love makes us its willing slaves. Love is God in us, who makes us rejoice in doing difficult feats of love and justice for Him. We are "slaves of God," Paul tells us in the sixth chapter of his letter to the Romans. And God is a "slave" of His Love for us.

Life is complicated, and in the end only the Church as a whole can help us discriminate between the true and false prophets, the good and evil spirits. We must cling together in our journey to God, else our bleached bones will be found lying in the deserts of heresy.

We have much to hope, and nothing to fear from change and the good prophets of change, if we hold with the Church, where God's Spirit speaks most resonantly. We can even hope that we will change one day to real Christliness, unable to rest complacent in a world of hungry and underprivileged people. I for one give witness of great need for change among us. When shall we change and hear Christ call: *I am hungry! Give me something to eat!*

23

Christian Witness

John the Baptist came to give witness to Christ. Though he wore "a garment of camel's hair," artists seem compelled to strip John naked. Why? What are they telling us about the prophetic witness? We want to unearth the answer because we share with John the prophetic role.

Our prophetic role actually has a perfection John's did not possess, as his enjoyed a perfection his predecessors' did not possess. The prophets preceding John foretold the coming of Christ. John revealed His presence. We reveal the success of His redemptive work.

From the way John witnessed we can clarify the way we ought to witness. We inherit, not his manner of life, but his spirit of life.

John disposed himself for his work by a total concentration on the Christ he was to reveal. Without wife or children or income or home or even an assured food supply, John was stripped of all ordinary human possessions and pursuits. His whole being and meaning were concentrated in his function.

John stands psychologically naked before us, and his very nakedness veils him. In stripping away his self-interest he strips his very self away. He becomes a window to the transcendent realities he came to reveal. He is reduced to a voice ringing out in the desert. He serves Christ in the service which no man can render to himself — the service of being praised and witnessed to and authenticated by another.

John gave witness to the very core of Jesus' meaning: "Behold the Lamb of God, the taker away of the sin of the world!" While the disciples needed the resurrection to discover Jesus' divinity, John sensed it from the very beginning: "I am not worthy to untie His sandal."

John's witness consisted in more than pointing to Christ. It pointed out that the only adequate preparation for Him was complete change of heart that entailed conversion to universal and practical love. "Anyone with two coats," John said, "must share with the man having none, and the one with something to eat must do the same."

John's conduct sharpens up our realization of the kind of witness we owe Christ. The obligation of Christian witness is not fulfilled by anything so cheap as an occasional act or word.

True Christian witness can only come out of what we are. We can be good witnesses of Christ only by being genuine disciples of Christ. The essence of Christian witness consists in the good life that is created day by day out of the Christian faith and love that burns within. "You will know them," Jesus said, "by their fruits."

The witness we give by Christian lives is true prophecy. It reveals God at work among us. It proves that the life of Christ is in us.

The bulk of Christly witness to the world must be given by the laity. They exercise their prophetic role primarily "by engaging in temporal affairs and by ordering them according to the plan of God" (Constitution on the Church).

Catholic consciences have often been imperfectly formed in childhood and have remained perpetually infantile. The result is the pervasive belief that religious worship and sexual purity constitute the essence of Catholic commitment to religion. The result in the world is godlessness: godlessness in education, in economic policies and in social mores. The result is not only godlessness in entertainment, but increasingly ungodly entertainment.

Do Catholics realize that they must bring God into life even at the cost of giving their lives? There is a sober lesson in the Greek word for witness, *martyria*. For Christians it came to mean *giving witness even to death,* and so we have the English word, martyr.

The Catholic family is the basic building block of Christian witness. The first ones the members witness to are one another. They reveal God to one another because they are made in His image and likeness. They reveal to one another their love for Christ and fidelity in Him. Out of this fidelity flows their faithfulness to one another and the indissolubility of their marriage.

It is instructive that through Malachi, the prophet of John's and Christ's coming, God condemned divorce as abhorrent. He also foretold that "Elijah to come" who was John, "would turn the hearts of fathers toward their children and the hearts of children toward their fathers." Love and reconciliation are signs of true witness.

No one can give adequate witness unless he has turned his heart from things to people. "By this will all men know you are my disciples," Jesus said, "if you have love for one another."

Nor can there be adequate witness without giving greater love to eternity than to time and to God than to man. One who succeeds in doing this is joyous, and unusually kind, and without anxiety. He is anchored to God in prayer, and so he has unshakable peace.

What faithful laity give witness to by these virtues of moderation and of transferred hope, faithful religious make more explicit. Religious priests, nuns and brothers testify by their vows to the "possession of heavenly goods here below." They are a living reminder to all Christians to put into practice their belief that "the People of God has no lasting city here below."

The prophetic role of laity and religious is made more firm by the prophetic role of the priest. He feeds their faith and love "by teaching, by sanctifying and by ruling with the authority of Christ."

Proclaiming Christ *is* the priest's work and his way of life. He proclaims the Good News most powerfully through the Eucharistic Sacrifice. There he not only announces the rising of Christ, but he calls the risen Christ bodily into the assembly.

Herein comes to light the most glorious effect of Christian witness. It not only proclaims Christ, but by disposing for Him, it brings Him.

24

Ways to Encounter God

One of my favorite childhood games was "Hide-and-Seek." While the "hunter" counted to twenty with eyes covered, everyone scurried into a hiding place, desperate with desire to be concealed before he heard the warning: "Ready or not, here I come!"

Strange how good games prepare us for life. Our relation with God is of Hunter and Hunted. Sometimes He hunts us, and sometimes we hunt Him.

Some of course deny there is any God, or any game of hide-and-seek. Others, fearing Him, always hide and never seek. Some seek Him and find Him. Others even bring Him.

All of these actors in the drama of religion played their role on the day Mary went to the temple to be purified (not because she needed it, but because she wanted to fulfill the Law). And in taking her Son with her she brought God to the temple.

"Suddenly there will come to the temple the Lord whom you seek," God announces through the prophet Malachi. "Yes, He is coming, says the Lord of Hosts, but who will endure the day of His coming, or who can stand when He appears? For He is like a refining fire." That is the question: *Who can stand when He comes?*

Mary can stand. Her "Yes" to His will brought Him into our flesh, into the "temple of His body." *The Holy Family can stand.* Their "Yes" to His will made manifest in the Law brought Him into the temple in Jerusalem. *Simeon can stand.* His "Yes" to the graces of longing and inspiration and prophecy brings God to the temples of our minds.

Then there are others who will not stand. "This Child," prophesies Simeon, "is set for the fall and for the rising of many in Israel."

There are those who will fall and those who will stand. We hope to be among those who will stand.

We hope to be like Simeon. Simeon resembles the man of Psalm 63: "O God, You are my God, I am seeking You, my soul is thirsting for You, my flesh is longing for You, a land parched, weary and waterless. I long to gaze on You." We hope, like Simeon, at last to gaze on God.

Christ comes into our lives in the liturgy, even as He came into Simeon's life in the temple of Jerusalem.

Christ first came into our lives at baptism. After the priest baptized us he gave us a lighted candle. Christ had just entered us, His new temples, and the burning light of our holy lives is the sign of His presence.

Gradually we were inducted into the other sacraments, further Christ-comings. Especially at the consecration of our Holy Sacrifice, God "comes suddenly into His temple." At Holy Communion, He enters the temple's inner sanctum, which we are.

The New Testament makes it clear that we are the new temple of God. We are the temple's "living stones," we are the temple of the body of Christ, where He dwells. Jesus Himself said: "He who eats My flesh and drinks My blood abides in Me and I in him."

In another place Jesus clearly promised to make us His temple: "If a man loves Me he will keep My word and the Father will love him and we will come to him and make our abode with him."

These words of promise include a muted warning. "Who shall stand when He appears?" *Only the man who loves Him enough to do His will.* The rebel does not love Christ and will not stand.

We were accordingly instructed at baptism: "If . . . you wish to enter life, keep the commandments."

Lying and false prophets abound today. They minimize sin.

They teach a corruptive permissiveness diametrically opposed to the revelation. They lead people to fall asleep in their sins and let the sacrament of penance collect dust. They spawn a people who cannot stand when God appears.

In his encyclical on the Mystical Body of Christ, Pius XII warned: "Let those, therefore, among the young clergy who make light of or weaken esteem of frequent confession realize that what they are doing is foreign to the Spirit of Christ, and disastrous for the Mystical Body of our Savior."

Christ taught, "If your eye leads you into sin, pluck it out!" He condemns the no-sin crowd with His warning against sin and unconditional condemnation of sin.

He warns us that the cost of following Him is constant vigilance. To build ourselves into His temples we must be like the Jews who returned from exile. They rebuilt their temple, with one hand on their weapons to ward off their enemies who were constantly trying to tear it down again.

Christ's own life and words make nonsense of those Christian teachers who no longer know the difference between good and evil themselves. The law of Christ is so clear in His own life He could say, not, "Try to understand," but, "Who can convict Me of sin?"

In his account of the presentation, Luke makes crystal clear the way to stand when God appears. *It is by doing His will.* The Holy Family were carrying out the *prescriptions of revelation.* Simeon was in the temple at the right moment because he obeyed the *promptings of the Spirit.*

Thus Luke underlines the two complementary sources of the knowledge of God's will: outer and inner, objective and subjective, outer teaching by the Church and inner guidance by the Spirit.

We need Luke's balanced emphasis in a day when freedom to follow our conscience is being corrupted into freedom to make decisions without recourse to authoritative sources of revelation and morality.

Scripture, tradition, the teaching Church, the laws of just government, the obligations of our state of life, are all ways in which God is manifesting His will. The man who rejects that will falls each time God appears.

Our obedient love invites Christ not to delay and to come

swiftly, finally and permanently into His living temples. In the three new Eucharistic prayers we voice our expectation: "Christ has died. Christ is risen. *Christ will come again."*

Christ will return in a transformed Eucharistic event that will make us His perpetual temples. Trent, quoting from Psalm 78, describes it by telling us that in heaven "the veils will be removed and they will partake of the same Bread of Angels that they now receive under the sacred species."

"They will see Him face to face," adds the Apocalypse, and "they will not need lamplight or sunlight, because the Lord God will be shining on them."

The candle of our baptism was the harbinger of the light of God's face for all of us.

25

The Parable of Hope

"A farmer," we find Jesus saying in the fourth chapter of Mark, "went out to sow." The scene appears peaceful, bucolic, devoid of excitement or conflict. But is it?

Actually this parable was generated in the crucible of conflict, and is fully intelligible only in the light of the conflict which produced it.

Mark records the turmoil preceding the parable. The teaching of Jesus had stirred a hornet's nest. The scribes were accusing Jesus of blaspheming. They even claimed He was in collusion with Satan. The Pharisees were plotting Jesus' destruction. Jesus' own relatives "set out to take charge of Him, convinced He was out of His mind."

What must have been the reaction of Jesus' own disciples to these disillusioning events? The kingdom of God was beginning to look like a mirage. John tells us in his Gospel that "many of His disciples left Him. . . ." His doctrine was too much for them.

What was the reaction of Jesus Himself to the raging controversies? In the words of John's Gospel, Jesus reacted by saying: "Stop complaining to each other. No one can come to Me unless he is drawn by the Father. . . ."

What was the reaction of Jesus to all the roadblocks men were setting up against the kingdom of God He was working to establish? *His answer was the parable of the sower.*

The prime emphasis of this parable is not on the doubtfulness of a good crop, but on the certainty of a good crop despite doubtful appearances.

God's business is like everything else. You have to know about it to judge its real progress, just as you have to know about growing things to make sound judgments about the expected crop.

Some people might think a microscopic mustard seed would never amount to anything — they might mistake it for a speck of dust — but lo, it grows more than six feet tall in a year! Some people might think a dab of yeast could amount to nothing; but lo, it leavens the whole batch of bread! *The kingdom of heaven is like that, too.*

Inexperienced people watching the farmer sowing the seed might chew their fingernails with concern (especially if they have invested their money in the crop) when they discover seed falling on pathways and rocks, and watch the birds come swooping in, after the farmer has finished, and start feeding on the newly planted seed.

The farmer would only laugh. His experienced eye sees that things are really quite promising. Identical circumstances prevailed in past years, and yet when late summer came, his fields were laden with produce.

The experienced eye of Jesus sees the promise, while the inexperienced eyes of others see only hopelessness. Jesus puts the promise He sees into a parable of hope. "And some fell on good soil, grew up, and yielded grain a hundred for one." *The rocks and the paths are barren at harvesttime, and so are the little weedy patches, but the whole field is a sea of grain.*

We need this parable in our age of worry. We cry with the Psalmist: "Awake, why are You asleep, O Lord?" *You are aware, Lord, of the world with its Gallup-poll mentality toward truth and morality. You know about the fifth column sowing evil seed in the Church. Why do You hide Your face?*

The Lord answers us with His parable of the sower. The lesson of the parable is that God will prevail. The attached explanation of the parable helps us understand that in this world even God's work is not supposed to proceed trouble-free. As a friend of mine likes to say, "Things are hopeless, but not serious!" It is in times of hopelessness that hope in God is born.

It would not do, however, to pass over the second lesson of the parable. We will prevail with God only if we make of ourselves good ground for the seed being planted.

"The seed is the word of God." Germination is by faith. The first hazard to avoid, then, is resistance to God's word. It is necessary to harrow the hard ground of our unbelief by asceticism.

"A child of God," Jesus said once, "listens to the word of God; if you refuse to listen, it is because you are not God's children." The alternative is to be the devil's children: "The devil is your father, and you prefer to do what your father wants."

Once the seed is in the ground, it can grow only if the soil is right for it. The soil can be made right only by divine means. In former ages men applied religion unwisely to usurp the role of natural causes; now we even more foolishly apply natural causes to usurp the role of religion.

There are no substitutes for the means Jesus has given us to make the word of God grow in us. Nothing can grow without the nourishment of prayer, the Mass, confession and communion, spiritual reading and good works.

If we do not use these means we remain rocky soil. "Without Me," Jesus said flatly, "you can do nothing." *Nothing.*

The battle with thorns and weeds is the law of life both in nature and in grace. When I was a novice, we used to be set to weeding during the silence of our retreats. When we returned to the same beds some months later in a subsequent retreat, the new crop of weeds always had a companion crop of old faults returned, to be rooted out again.

In nature, there are such things as the witchweed. Its microscopic seeds lie dormant, even for years, waiting for a host. As soon as a host plant grows nearby, the witchseed germinates, attaches itself, and eats at the life of the tender new plant.

In human life we can let ourselves be eaten away by all the parasitic forms of life which have nothing to do with real life: remember, the soil need not be bad to choke out true life.

The answer to all the witchweeds of human life is the daily examination of conscience. An unexamined life is not worthy living, for it soon goes over to weeds. Surveying our life daily compels us to practice the asceticism of right choice.

Work is not enough unless it includes good works; reading is dissipation unless it embraces spiritual reading; socialization is banal unless it includes socializing with God in prayer. *For concentration on the pleasures of this life is enough to shut out Christ-life.*

"Fear not, little flock, for it is your Father's good pleasure to give you the kingdom. Sell your possessions and give alms . . . and be like men who are waiting for their master to come home. . . ."

26

Authority: Our Firmest Hope

We human beings are voyagers through time and space, yet so complex are we that simultaneously our inner selves have a sense of being adrift upon the uncharted seas of eternity. Mysteriously, we are there without a compass, unable ever to find the way unless given authoritative guidance.

It is alarming, then, when authority comes to have a nasty ring in men's ears. Authority is, basically, the prerogative of God alone. "Neither be called masters, for you have one master, the Christ."

Still, Christ rules through certain men who exercise His authority by His own appointment: "I will give you the keys of the kingdom of heaven, and whatever you bind upon earth shall be bound in heaven, and whatever you loose upon earth shall be loosed in heaven." Christ also sanctioned secular authority: "Render to Caesar what is Caesar's."

There is no doubt that the authority delegated by God has been abused by men. It is a vicious crime. "I know of no greater sin," said Mahatma Gandhi, "than to oppress the innocent in the name of God."

Misuse of delegated authority has clouded the grandeur of God's own authority, and stained its goodness. Yet God's delegated authority remains necessary to us. In fact, a good leader is one of God's great blessings. Think of America's yearning for a capable leader at this time. Wonder a little, too, whether we are worthy of one after the way we abuse our leaders.

Even in the Church we find rebellious juvenile attitudes toward obedience and authority — as though authority were a set of taboos of which the mature must be rid.

In particular there is a hue and cry over imagined attacks on freedom of conscience, as though authoritative guidance were oppression. Actually, freedom of conscience is simply the power and the responsibility to make right judgments concerning truth and conduct. It includes the responsibility to accept authoritative definitions of right conduct. The conscience passionately in search of truth longs for authoritative guidance, for it rarely can find the way unerringly by itself.

At root, authority is the authentic channel through which God, the highest Reality and the divine Author of our being, invites us or compels us along the way by which we can participate most abundantly in reality. It is the Manufacturer giving the operating specifications for His product.

The highest Authority is the Author of life. He tailored life. He gave it direction. He is its only authoritative Guide, for He alone can lead us through life without plunging into the crevasses of error or straying into psychic hinterlands where the guide and the guided discover only that they have lost themselves.

He who knows what is in man, and loves everything authentic about man, is our loved guide. He established His authority by incontrovertible signs. By forgiving sins He laid claim to complete authority over the condition of the relationship between God and man. By miraculously healing bodies He gave corroborative evidence of His claimed power to heal souls.

These actions of Jesus are revelation, that is, they are God revealing. It was most fitting that Jesus reveal by actions as well as by words. I say this not simply because the actions were needed to substantiate the words, but because the compassionate actions reveal the heart of Jesus Himself, and that is the heart of revelation.

The Scriptures teach us throughout how grateful we ought to be to God because God has been so good to us. I enter a plea that we prayerfully reflect on how grateful we should be for all legitimate authority, which descends from the Father through the Son.

The authority of God is the motive for our faith and the guide of our actions. Fight it directly or indirectly as it exists in His delegates, and we sabotage the foundations of our own saving faith. When we believe in His revelation, we are really bowing to His authority over truth. When we are obedient to His directives, we are really loving His authorship of our being.

We would deeply love genuine authority if we understood that God's authority is the kind of authority that being is. A sane man doesn't argue with reality. He doesn't argue with a stone because it has the qualities it has. A sane man accepts reality, and to be able to do that is one of the clearest marks of maturity. To accept God's authority is to accept reality.

God's authority is the authority of reality. His words are revelation. His commands are interwoven with the very stuff of existence. Following them is growth and discovery and destiny.

We should be eager for God's authoritative guidance wherever He offers it, even through His delegates or vicars. We must have patience with their faults, as they must have patience with ours whom they guide. If we only remembered the alternative of drifting without compass on the sea of eternity, we would lustily "praise God for having bestowed such authority on men."

27

Christianity Unfenced

A lady Baptist and I were conversing peacefully about faith in Christ when abruptly she asked: "Have you been saved?"

"I don't know exactly what you intend by that," I responded, "but I've been baptized."

"I don't care if you've been baptized a hundred times! Have you been saved?" She glared at me and I at her as the tide of ecumenism palpably receded.

"Well, thank God," I suddenly exclaimed, "that we agree on so much!" We smiled and the ecumenical dialogue proceeded.

Ecumenism is the movement in which Christians labor to produce the unity that Jesus prayed for on the night of the Last Supper. He it is who launched the ecumenical movement. He has sheep outside the fold, He tells us, but His heart is set on the day when all shall be united. "Then there will be one flock, one Shepherd."

Jesus yearned for this unity. The night before He died Jesus gave us the Eucharist, the sacrament of unity. He prayed, too, for all His members, "that they all may be one; even as You, Father, are in Me, and I in You, that they also may be in us. . . ."

Vatican II was true to the heart of Jesus when it made the work for Christian unity "one of the chief concerns of the Council."

Ecumenism is the struggle to comprehend the unsuspected magnitude of our unity in Christ, and to dislodge every remaining wall of separation. The walls of separation are the obvious part of the iceberg. It is the nine-tenths of our common bond lying unseen beneath the sound and fury of our disagreements that love and faith must bring to the surface of our awareness.

Unity's spearhead will never be doctrine, but always persons — men and women who see beyone the morass of our differences to our superabounding oneness in Christ.

The late Father Gus Weigel, S.J., was one of those men who lived on the cutting edge of that spearhead. He never minimized difference, yet he personified unity. His hope was "not conversion, not compromise, but convergence." He saw where the unity is and where it remains to be sought — in the mystery of Christ and His Church.

The great problem is that the Church is a mystery. The great hope stems from the fact that recent Popes and the Second Vatican Council and the World Council of Churches as well as other Protestant and Catholic ecumenists have penetrated the mystery more deeply and discerned more clearly the hidden parts of the iceberg *and the hidden unity of what appeared to be separate icebergs.*

Protestant witness and service and work in Scripture have clamored to be seen and accepted for what they are — genuine works of Christ, and of members and ecclesial communities truly belonging to Him.

Christ works sometimes with us, sometimes despite us. The ecumenical movement surged up out of the secret works of the Spirit and took most of us by surprise — but it should have been a most pleasant surprise, for it is a new hurricane of the wind of the Spirit sweeping away fences that men have built on God's own territory.

Time for amazement, however, is long past. Time for our cooperation has long been present. The Decree on Ecumenism "exhorts all the Catholic faithful to recognize the signs of the times and to participate skillfully in the work of ecumenism."

What can we do to promote unity? Oneness can come only from living the one truth under the one Shepherd. Everything that promotes renewal and reform of our faith and our life in Christ transfuses new life into the movement for unity.

The Decree on Ecumenism counsels us to eliminate "words, judgments and actions" which in any way impugn our separated brethren. It invites competent theologians of the various communions to resolve differences without violating anyone's faith or convictions. It invites us to work together where we can agree already, as in social problems and missions of mercy; and to arrange occasions to pray together to both express and seek unity.

As never before the Church confesses openly that without the other sheep she herself is impoverished. Would not her children have been better nourished with the word of God if the flock had remained one and the separated brethren had done their rich scriptural work in union with us? And would not the brethren have been better nourished with the Bread of the Eucharist and better guided toward oneness of truth and love if they had not gone their own way? Their separation is both their wound and ours.

We need more dialogue, Cardinal Suenens asserts, while we all keep a grip in the meantime on our faith and our sense of humor. He insistently reminds us that dialoguing includes listening. He suggests "that we follow the proportion which nature has indicated by giving us two ears and only one mouth."

Ecumenical experts seek more open-house days in the Churches, and more living-room dialogues. Families and family apostolic groups have scope for urgent action here. It is on this grass-roots level that we need more enthusiasm for what Christ desires. It would be easy and natural to invite Protestant friends into CFM and Christian Life Community meetings when they deal with apostolic works in the neighborhood which could be more effectively conducted by a consortium of all faiths. Cooperation on the family level is so important that some feel it is there the movement for oneness will live or die.

The corporate activity that arises from these talks is central to ecumenical progress. In 1952 the Lund Conference on Faith and Order asked: "Should not the Churches act together in all matters except those in which deep differences of conviction compel them to act separately?"

We must be responsibly alert to the danger of doctrinal infractions, but most leading ecumenists are bent on promoting oneness *in Christ and the Church He envisioned,* not outside them. They know that divisions were engendered in the first place by seriously misunderstanding or grossly abandoning Christ's teaching. They know that unity can be achieved not by abandoning our convictions in Christ, but by mutually examining their validity, purifying them and living them.

We Catholics must neither underestimate what we have to gain from the separated brethren nor forget what we have to give them. Individual Catholics have not been very faithful to scriptural reading. Let us begin now. A few verses read before family meals, especially from the Gospels, would do much to develop love of God's word in both children and parents. So let us begin it. It is a work both of religion and of unity.

Catholics have been faithful to the Eucharistic mystery. Let us continue to be. There, in the Pasture of Life to which the one Shepherd devotedly leads us, lies the most authentic hope for unity.

PART FOUR

28

The Anawim

While Sambo was at prayer the Lord directed him to take up residence in a certain affluent neighborhood and join the congregation there. He tried, but the realtor would not sell, and the pastor told him he must have garbled God's message. Sambo prayed again, and returned to the pastor with the report: "The Lord said: 'It's all right, Sambo. I've been trying to get in that church for a long time myself!'"

Life's drama is often droll and often tragic, but God teaches life's innocent sufferers laughter. "Happy are you when people abuse you and persecute you and speak all kinds of calumny against you on My account. Rejoice and be glad, for your reward will be great in heaven. This is how they persecuted the prophets before you."

Even upon those in the mainstream of salvation revelation, however, it only dawned slowly that suffering injustice from the powerful without doing violence in return but also without ceasing to give witness to them was a blessed work.

Early wisdom literature chooses to mention the lazy poor, the castoffs who pull ruin down around their own ears. The prophets, however, came to see and proclaim that the poor and humble folk, the *anawim,* deserve help, not condemnation. They are often good and simple men disadvantaged and oppressed and crushed and rendered impotent by the gradual subtraction of their human rights in favor of the powerful and the affluent who have no intention of compromising their advantage by reversing the process in behalf of justice.

Taught in the school of lifelong obedience and humble service to their masters, the poor and oppressed learned rather easily to obey God's commands too. In consequence the poor came to be thought of as the chosen ones still faithful to God, the elect remnant among rebellious men, the favored ones for whom God has stored up His saving future.

Finally, the poor of God came to be identified as the people who — whether rich or poor — count God as their all and obey Him in all, and count everything else as nothing because they hope all from Him.

The Suffering Servant foretold by Isaiah is the exemplary Poor Man of God. So pleasing to God is He, and so useful in God's plan, that He and His suffering are the source of salvation for many.

Jesus was that Suffering Servant of God, rejected by men. Neither politically powerful nor independently wealthy, He was judged and condemned and destroyed by the false court of the powerful and the affluent who refused to allow their hegemony to be challenged by a financial and political no-account.

At the Last Supper Jesus assured His disciples that the world's judgment against the oppressed would be reversed by the Holy Spirit, the new Advocate He would send them. Jesus had to depart the world in the death which the world inflicted as its judgment against Him, but He foretold His return in the resurrection-life which is the judgment of God against the world. Further, our new divine Advocate, by His works in us, continues to reverse the judgment the world continues to make.

We men are in the end judged by our own judgments. Some men were judged by their judgment of the Son of God born of the Virgin Mary. Most of us are being judged by our judgment of the sons of God born of Adam.

St. James says flatly: "My brothers, do not try to combine faith in Jesus Christ, our glorified Lord, with the making of distinctions between classes of people." By denying our brotherhood in word or evading it in action we deny God's fatherhood of all.

Jesus promised us victory through God's reversal of the world's materialistic judgments in ongoing history. What constitutes the judgment is the good the Holy Spirit brings forth in us. The danger always remains, however, that we will align ourselves with worldly judgments and be condemned with them.

Not the name but the actions make the Christian and the worldling. All are Christ's who stand with Him in working to join men in one fellowship and one common good under God. Those are the world's who stand against this oneness for any reason.

A recent poll claimed that churchgoers are more likely to condemn the poor for their underprivileged state than non-churchgoers. Ugly rumors are circulating about pastors who "protect" their parishioners from the "inroads" of blacks — thus depriving one class of human beings of their just rights in order to provide the other class with unjust insurance against financial loss. If the charges are true, these are corruptors of Christianity who "do good" if it costs them nothing, but will not even do justice if it costs them something.

Some Christians are inflamed with rage when the churches make just social demands upon their consciences. If they will read the letter of St. James, they can find the saving counsel to "humbly welcome the revelation that has struck its roots into you, that has the power to save your souls." James also tells us that "a man's anger does not accomplish God's just purpose."

I have seen Christians outraged at the slowness of "law and order" to crush out the riots among the dispossessed. If it is justice they love, why are they not equally outraged by the slowness of law and order to correct the systematic injustices which society allows to pile up against the poor?

The "National Advisory Commission of Civil Disorders" pointed out the painful experience of ghetto dwellers. They find civil authorities lack funds and personnel to attend to their grievances except in the most agonizingly slow fashion. Yet these same authorities find adequate funds to police them twenty-four hours a day. So they wonder if "law" maintains "order" or only existing conditions.

The Christ of the resurrection joins us into one people through His Eucharistic mystery. That mystery should rush us back to our communities "eager for noble deeds," especially the deed of dismantling the walls of division that have made men forget they are brothers and sons of God. Without that brotherhood we are all poor, but not the poor of God. With it we are all rich, the rich children of God.

29

Our New Neighbors

Is it true, as some think, that Christianity's helmsmen have become so bogged down over the question of right and left that they are no longer teaching right and wrong? Or is it rather true that the question of right and left is often actually the question of right and wrong?

Is an American's stand on foreign aid simply a matter of politics, or is it a matter of religion? Is a man's position on the racial issue a matter of free choice or a matter of right and wrong? Along with many other Churchmen I opt for the second choice.

The whole issue is the issue of updating the concept of neighbor to accord with the updating of civilization itself. Because human society is developing vaster and more intricate relationships, so must the concept of neighbor.

St. Luke tells us in his tenth chapter about a lawyer who was aware 2,000 years ago of the ongoing problem of saying who our neighbor is. The lawyer stated admirably that the essence of religion is not a set of rules for playing life like a game, but a heart of love that moves spontaneously to do what is needed.

The lawyer knew this speculatively and put it brilliantly when he said we must love God without limit and our neighbor as ourselves. Then he spoiled everything by asking: "Who is my neighbor?"

The Jewish law taught the lawyer that even the stranger living among the Jews had to be treated with love and consideration. The law, however, did not spell out the whole spectrum of human interrelationships. No written law can.

Jesus responded to the question by telling the parable of the Good Samaritan. Jesus showed that the neighbor cannot be circumscribed by place or nationality. He taught that love is not a national but an international force for good.

In the third chapter of his letter to the Corinthians, St. Paul sheds further light on the good neighbor policy by contrasting the ministry of the Old Law with that of the Law of Christ. Even the ministry of the Old Law was glorious, but how much more glorious is the ministry of the New Law!

The guiding principle of the new ministry is not a set of words that can be encrusted with obsolescence, but the Spirit of Love who breathes new life into each situation. If we have this Spirit, how can we fail to recognize a brother simply because he is cloaked in a different skin? What will we do if the Spirit one day calls upon us to recognize a brother in the flesh of an alien species?

In his first letter to the Corinthians, we find Paul promoting a charitable enterprise of international dimensions. He is taking up a collection from the people of Corinth in Asia Minor in order to bring relief to the destitute in Jerusalem.

To stimulate Corinthian generosity Paul tells how the Macedonians responded: "Somehow, in most difficult circumstances, their joy and the fact of being down to their last penny themselves, produced a magnificent concern for other people."

Paul reminds the Corinthians of the Model of all givings: "Do you remember the generosity of Jesus Christ, the Lord of us all? He was rich beyond our telling, yet He became poor for your sakes so that His poverty might make you rich."

What Paul was trying to teach his Corinthians the Second Vatican Council was trying to teach us. It met to bring our Christian ministry more into harmony with the needs of today's world. It was concerned with updating our concept of neighbor and it was determined to update our ways of serving him.

That is why, throughout such documents as the Constitution on the Church in the Modern World, and the Decree on the Apostolate of the Laity, the emphasis is not on serving the man living next door, but men living everywhere. And so we are reminded in these documents of our Christian responsibility for the shape our culture is taking, and for the laws and the organizations burgeoning within it. We are our brother's keeper, and our brother is everywhere.

Concerning international solidarity, Pope Paul wrote in "The Progress of Peoples": "It is time for all men and all peoples to face up to their responsibilities.

"Let each one examine his conscience," he continued. "Is he prepared to support out of his own pocket works and undertakings organized in favor of the most destitute? Is he ready to pay higher taxes so that the public authorities can intensify their efforts in favor of development?"

Pope Paul asks whether the young are ready to leave their country, if necessary, in the effort to "assist in this development of the young nations."

Since most of us do not live next door to poor men, we have got to update the meanings of the counsels of love to make them mean what they ought to mean today.

Today they ought to mean something like this: "I was hungry in Asia, and you wrote your Congressmen in support of the foreign aid program. I was thirsty, and you joined the Peace Corps to build a dam. I was sick and you supported Medicare legislation. I was naked and you shipped me your extra clothing."

Two men were watching television. They saw the starving and the underprivileged in many places. One man flipped the dial. The other wrote a check to the Bishops' Relief Fund.

Which of the two was neighbor to man?

30

Honesty

In some unidentified place Jesus purged an evil spirit from a man and restored his power of speech. For thanks, certain bystanders condemned His good action as evil. They accused Him of conniving with the devil to put on a show of goodness (Lk. 11:14f).

Jesus launched a devastating attack against the specious arguments of His accusers by giving norms for judging the good and evil of human actions. We badly need those norms today. We live in an age when many good things are condemned as evil, and some evil things are fobbed off as good, and some people do destructive things with a good motive.

In making our judgments, we ought to remember that there is one basic difference between the habitually good man and the habitually evil man. The former is honest and the second is a liar. The former faces up to truth whatever the cost, and the latter lies to his own soul rather than pay the cost.

The good man arrives at his judgment of goodness by the help of unfettered reason and the word of God and the guidance of the Spirit. The evil man judges those things to be good which advance his own vested interests.

Not that the evil man is always consciously lying to himself.

After a while there may be no need for conscious lies. Man is a deep pit, and with practice can draw out of the depths judgments to suit his convenience. Scripture has long attested to this, and now those who have lain on the psychiatrists' couches can confirm it.

"Woe," cried Isaiah, "to those who call evil good and good evil, who put darkness for light and light for darkness. . . ."

The good man has the gift of spiritual sight and speech, but the evil man is blind and dumb. He is blind because he can no longer see truth; he is dumb because though he spew out a torrent of words, they are vitiated by untruth; they are *no-words,* for words are vehicles of truth. He is sick with a gutted conscience, which is the wound one's own lies and evil inflict on the self.

All of us have both inherited and inflicted wounds upon the inner self. God willing, they are not blinding, but still they may befog our perception. Most of us seem capable, through our snap judgments supporting our own unexamined convictions, of condemning the Holy Spirit and His best cooperators.

We had better take warning — even alarm — from the recorded fact that the Son of God was accused of diabolic collaboration by men who presumably considered themselves fervently devoted to God.

Some Catholics blindly condemn almost all change; some blindly condemn those who refuse to permit almost all things to change; some seem blind to the holiness of the Church and condemn it almost as though it were evil.

Undoubtedly the Church's members, priestly, religious and lay people, are highly imperfect in some instances. Undoubtedly prophets have been sent in the past to castigate God's people. But physicians blinded by their own excesses are not to be trusted with the scalpel. Christ gave the norm for those who would exact justice: "Let him who is without sin cast the first stone." One of the most diabolical things about most ecclesial criticism is that it condemns one class (usually bishops nowadays), thus dividing the Church against itself.

It is about time we all remembered that accusing another either falsely or without necessity is still a particularly devilish kind of sin. Love hides the faults of another. We all have the responsibility of contesting such accusations, because we are our brothers' keepers.

"Do not let anyone deceive you," Paul wrote the Ephesians, "by worthless arguments."

Paul's own argument for honest conduct, given in that same letter, is that we are called to be like little children artlessly imitating our bigger brother Christ. We are supposed to parade around in His footsteps of love. He never criticized us, even though He died for our misdeeds. He reserved His condemnation for those whose misrepresentations led innocent people into sin.

Christlike honesty leaves no room for the lie that makes drunkenness something manly and lewd talk something sophisticated, and indecent dress something stylish, and cheating business deals something to brag about. Love "sees no fun in wickedness."

Our judgments against evil can be sharpened and confirmed by turning to the arguments Jesus marshalled against His lying accusers.

Jesus' first argument undermines His accusers' whole line of argument. How can His works be in collusion with the devil when His works are toppling the whole reign of the devil? (This argument counsels us to support as far as possible any one doing anything constructive for integration, for peace, for the poor, etc., even though we do not like the way they go about it. Pope Paul led the way when he praised the spirit of the youth who made himself a fiery torch for freedom, but asserted that we do not believe man has the right to take his own life for any cause.)

Jesus' second argument draws on a comparison between Himself and other Jews who have cast out devils. If such other Jews were considered to be holy men working by God's power, what was the reason for denying that Jesus cast out devils by the same power? His accusers could not give any reason for such biased judgment.

Jesus' third argument is that only one stronger than the owner of a house can overpower him and seize his house. Since Jesus is overpowering Satan and seizing his strongholds, it must mean that Jesus is, or comes from one, stronger than Satan. That has to be God.

The fourth argument is that those who undo Jesus' works are not on His side. But clearly Satan is struggling to undo His works. Then, contrary to the allegations, Satan is not on His side nor He on Satan's.

The fifth point Jesus makes is really a warning. He is emptying men of evil, but unless they invite the Spirit in to fill them with good, the vacuum in them will suck in a flood of evil, leaving them worse than ever.

Finally, Jesus puts His finger on the true source of human goodness and blessedness. To the woman who called His Mother happy in her Motherhood, Jesus said: "Shall we not say, 'Blessed are those who hear the word of God and keep it'?" Neither Mary, nor even Jesus, could presume on their unique relationship to God. Jesus had shown by His arguments that, contrary to His detractors' allegations, all signs confirmed the fact that He was wholly God's man, doing only His will.

We find Jesus and His Church giving us many norms of truth and goodness. We will not accept them, however, unless we already love Jesus and can say with Paul, "I know Whom I have believed." Nor will we persevere in them unless we learn with the psalmist that doing God's will is an experience sweeter than eating bees' honey.

Delight in the Father's will and love of Jesus give us the courage to renounce our lies of convenience and, open-eyed and face-to-face, welcome truth as a friend.

31

Lived Religion

A serious split is developing among Christians about the nature of their religion. Some feel that the hour of worship should bring them the consolations of God, and a period of respite from the entanglements of the world. Others, usually headed by a contingent from among the clergy, insist Christianity is a way of life, not an escape from life.

The latter refuse to divorce religion and life. Their focus is not on the Christian in the temple but the Christian in the world. They hold that the body of Christians who want to segregate Christianity from the social issues have emasculated Christianity.

This is an issue worth examining. At the root of the matter is the fact that Jesus has taken bodily departure from history, and Christians await His second coming. What should be our way of life in this interim time?

Two facts in particular bear on the answer we make to that question. The first fact is that almost 2,000 years have underlined Jesus' assertion that only the Father knows the time of His second coming.

We must, therefore, live in this interim time as though Jesus may return during our lifetimes, and as though He may not. We must in consequence plan for both the future of humanity and for the future of Christianity.

The second pertinent fact concerns the meaning of Christ's second coming. Is He coming again primarily for the purpose of the general judgment? The second coming is commonly presented in that light, but it is a false emphasis, though an understandable one. Actually, the central purpose of Christ's return is to reclaim the universe in power for Himself and His people. The general judgment is only a necessary prelude to that finalizing of His triumph.

This emphasis on the true purpose of Christ's second coming illuminates the meaning of the interim time. *It is the time of the continuation of the Incarnation.* It is the period during which His members are being born, maturing and carrying on His work. It is the epoch during which the whole universe is being reclaimed from sin and disorder and cosmic immaturity. It is the span of history during which Christ's victory is being extended by His members in preparation for His majestic return.

Many people seem never quite able to grasp the fact that, despite appearances, the Creator has not surrendered even the least sector of His creation to the rule of sin and disorder. He is in fact reasserting His hegemony over the whole domain of creation which has fallen under the sway of sin. Not with the iron fist of massive power is He doing this, but with the gentle strength of the Incarnation.

The role of the faithful is not only to submit to His rule, but to extend it, through the course of history, into the whole life and work of man. Those are certainly right who insist Jesus called His followers to live Christianity as a way of life, not as an escape from life.

Christian escapists are throwbacks to the non-revealed religions which sought to flee history instead of filling up history by conquering self-rebelliousness and all the forces resistant to man, and laying all at the feet of the Creator at the end of time.

Those who preach the Good News and administer the baptism of the Kingdom will, Christ said, "lay their hands on the sick, who will recover." The love Christ brought inevitably works for a total rebirth of man — spiritual, mental, moral and physical. A healthy universe is the only one worthy of Him.

Those who give primacy to the Christian in the world and not in the temple are, however, wrong in the end. Those who put the world first, end up worldlings. The Christian's relation to God always comes first, and Jesus always taught this. And we find in the first letter of John this criterion of our fidelity to our religion: "By this we know that we love the children of God, when we love God and obey His commandments. For this is the love of God, that we keep His commandments." We cannot be effective in serving our neighbor if we do not first serve God.

Jesus forewarned us of the sufferings to come upon us for putting God first: persecution and martyrdom. "And they will do such things because they never knew the Father nor Me." The difficulty arises from the fact that we bring the knowledge of the true God into a world which prefers to fashion its own gods, and has always slain the prophets for upholding something greater than itself.

Yet only when the primacy is given to God can we hope to accomplish anything lasting for man. "Without Me," Jesus said, "you can do nothing." God alone is the adequate and authoritative Architect of the universe.

Sin is the attempt to set up dissident centers of cosmic architecture. The atheist insists there is no cosmic Architect but man. The deist insists that God has created, but thereupon left all things in man's hands to be settled by human reason alone. The Christian theist maintains that in Christ God has capped His plan of creation, and only by cooperating with His revealed plan can we avoid working at cross-purposes with the Lord of history.

"Trade until I come," one of the characters says in a parable of Jesus. The lesson of the parable is that we are responsible for sensible use of the personal gifts and endowments each of us has from God. Each of us is an integrated part of the pattern of creation. We are not our own. *If our very selves do not belong to us, how much less does our property?* All is held in trust, to be used for God, His purposes and His people.

"When one of you speaks, let it be like the things said by God," Peter instructs us in his first letter; "when one of you shares, let it be as from the resources which God provides." Christ ascended, but remained behind in us, His other selves doing His work still.

Many Christians have as yet hardly dreamed of the obligation they have to God and man. When they awaken to their responsibilities, and live up to them, they will indeed come singing to the Holy Sacrifice, because they will find there more than a respite and a consolation. They will find the God of consolations and they will enter consciously into the mystery of the conquest of history.

32

Responsibility

Five thousand men were hungry when Jesus asked: "Where shall we ever buy bread for them to eat?" Nowadays 180 million children under fourteen are chronically hungry. Who shall provide bread for them? Shall God or man?

Let us battle it out with God. Whose job is it, His or ours? Who ought to close the gap between human expectation and human existence? And what is the source of the gap? Happily, John's account of the miraculous feeding of 5,000 points toward some answers.

Jesus fed the men, but when they wanted to make Him king, He fled. He expected their reaction. He knew His people wanted to make of their religion a source of easy living. Whenever He was ready to turn stones to bread His tumultuous reception was assured.

Today many believers use their religion as an excuse for doing nothing for others. They believe there is a God. They leave others to His care. They set out to fulfill themselves as discrete units, as individuals, or families, or (if they are a little more largehearted) as nations.

This is the wrong answer to the questions raised above. It is the first source of the gap between human expectations and human existence. No man is an island. No nation is an island. No nation will ever be without serious problems as long as one nation has serious problems.

Our problem is of overdeveloped self-centeredness and underdeveloped mutual concern. Religion counters this lopsidedness. The first thing religion does is to make us recognize we are brothers. "No man ever despised his own flesh," and we are one flesh. The second thing religion teaches us is to be responsible for our brother. *The attitude of the murderer is:* "Am I my brother's keeper?"

These false attitudes toward other men come from a false attitude toward religion. Religion is not a magic substitute for the use of our own powers and our own responsibilities. Nor is it, on the other hand, merely a second-rate organization to have around in order to fill in the gaps of service left by civil government.

Religion is our relationship with God. True religion tells us of our godlike powers and commands us to use them to fullfill our godlikeness: "Fill the earth and conquer it."

What is within the compass of human power is human work. Feeding man is man's work. The atheist knows this. The believer had better not forget it, or he is worse than the atheist.

No good pagan has ever been indifferent to hungry flesh — of man or beast. The Christian is called to far greater compassion and far greater activity in feeding the hungry. To the motive of his solidarity with all flesh is added his motive of being co-worker with God.

Feeding the hungry is a parent's responsibility. God recognizes His Father's role, but He has entrusted it to mankind. Scripture recognized God as the One who cares for the orphan and the widow, the hungry and the poor. Scripture also recognizes that mankind is God's helpmate, and that it is the godly man who does God's work.

It was as man that Jesus fed the 5,000. He was doing man's work, which we are to imitate. Someone might argue that that might be true, but that the manner in which Jesus fed them was God's manner. *My answer is that the manner in which we feed the hungry must also be God's manner.* If we consistently feed the hungry out of brotherly concern, that is a greater miracle than the physical miracle Jesus employed. That is *a moral miracle, a miracle of love*. It was of such things that Jesus said: "Whoever believes in Me will perform the same works that I do myself; he will perform even greater works."

We live in a world of hungry human flesh, and it is as men that we must feed them. What can stir us out of our business-as-usual attitude?

Inhabitants of a world in crisis, we have let our foreign aid program dwindle. We used to allocate just over one percent of our national income. Over the last fifteen years we have let that percentage shrink to about half of what it was.

We have grown understandably tired of helping others, but we cannot afford the luxury of such inhuman fatigue. The children are still starving to death, and not in Biafra alone. LAB (Latin America Bureau) reports the tragedy of our own international neighbors. In Brazil one of five infants dies in its first year. In some areas, forty percent die. Poverty of human resources is the problem. In some Latin American countries nearly ninety percent are illiterate.

These things need not be, and they need not continue, and they will not continue if we live as Christians responding to the crisis, and adjusted to the fact that not one act but a lifetime of acts is called for by all of us. No one is too small to help — not even our children — and certainly no one is too big.

There are things we can do. We can begin by realizing that this job belongs at least as much to the laity as to the priests and bishops. Priests must do all they can to awaken responsibility and to nourish Christlikeness, but the laymen and laywomen are the ones possessed of the necessary expertise. They must also manifest the necessary heroism of commitment.

We can begin by sending a donation to the United States Bishops' Latin America Bureau.

We can support increased foreign aid for underdeveloped nations by letters to our Congressional representatives. We can learn about PAVLA (Papal Volunteers for Latin America), and either volunteer or at least propagate the information for the benefit of those who can. The Church needs lay missionaries, including married teams, to work alongside priests and nuns around the world.

We could set up a "sister city program" with a city in an underdeveloped nation. If established on a parish-to-parish basis, the program would encourage the two peoples to become personally involved with one another so that not only services but love could be interchanged. The Second Vatican Council called for such aid between Churches. It also called for every Christian home to be an apostolic training ground for the children. Even the children could be trained to skip dessert occasionally so the savings could go to hungry children overseas.

When we have done all we can, the gap between man's expectations and his existence will still be large. That makes us turn back to religion and to Christ.

Jesus fed the 5,000 because to give the bread that *supports* life is man's task. He fed them miraculously because to supply bread that *gives* life is God's task, and Jesus wanted to indicate symbolically that the Father was standing by to complete His task. The miracle of the bread foreshadowed the first Easter, on which the Father would send into the world the risen Jesus to be our bread of life.

33

God's Place in Religion

A knight of the road happened on the revival just as the preacher asked who wanted to go to heaven. The latecomer alone failed to raise a hand in assent, so the preacher glared at him and demanded: "Don't you want to go to heaven?" "O!" exclaimed the itinerant, shooting up his hand, "I thought you said, 'Right now!' "

How do *we* feel when we read the Gospel accounts of Jesus' prophecy about the end of the world? It is clear that Jesus wants us to realize that life must be lived with our eyes focused on its final meaning. Not events in life but life itself is the religious event.

Religion begins and ends with God. Religion turns us toward God, but revealed religion doesn't begin with man at all. Revealed religion is initiated by God pronouncing His inviting word, is responded to by our reception of His word in faith, and ends by our receiving God Himself in love.

There are many misuses of religion. Religion can be prostituted to serve as a prop for the *status quo*. It can be used as a mere means of improving human conduct. It can be debased into a narcissistic spiritual self-saving activity, replete with spiritual gymnastics and spiritual health foods and fads.

It can be used as a lever by the sociologists to pry out of people the kind of mutual concern that men ought to have for one another. It can be twisted by Gnostics into a class society where only the intellectual elite possess the means of salvation.

Today's Church is struggling to ward off many of these perversions of religion. One of the worst is the pretense that the words of salvation flow from the pens of the most recent scholars rather than from the saving deeds of Jesus accepted in faith.

What all these perversions of religion share in common is a turning away from God. God is extruded from religion. The consequence is that Jesus' talk of an end-time to history is treated as sheer myth.

Paul was fighting some of these perversions in his letter to the Colossians. Paul lays stress on the only saving knowledge, that which comes from God, who gives us salvation through His Son. And Paul stresses the fact that we must not only believe but live the faith.

It is only when we throw on the junkheap every man-made form of salvation insinuated into our religion by someone or other and look to God's doing that we begin to raise our eyes toward the goal God has set for us. *Only after we jettison the idea that religion is a matter of doing and open ourselves to the awareness that it is really a matter of friendship, do we begin to look to the time the Friend will appear to cement our fellowship forever.* Only then do we look on the end of this world as a promise, not a threat.

Paul sets the Christian attitude toward death and the death of time. He admits to the Corinthians that he does not want to be stripped of his body by death, but he does long to have his body clothed over with the new life of Christ that the resurrection will bring.

Paul reaches the high water mark of Christian fearlessness in his letter to the Philippians. Gladly would he be temporarily separated from his body to be joined with Christ the sooner. There is only one drawback. His people still need him, and he is willing to remain in exile for their sakes.

We have to try to share Paul's attitude. Our interest in the affairs of time must be tempered by our expectation of going to Christ. Jesus Himself warned us that those who are possessed by wealth find it practically impossible to make the pilgrim journey to

God. Jesus called some followers to deliberate poverty and permanent celibacy to remind all followers that neither the world nor man is the meaning of man. God is.

Paul wrote the Corinthians that they must moderate their attachment to everything, even marriage. "Those who have to deal with the world," he added, "should not become engrossed in it. I say this because the world as we know it is passing away."

Jesus Himself reduces to several points the practical consequences of the prophecy concerning the world's end. He does it in parables following on the prophecy.

In the parable of the good servant, He praises fidelity and warns us not to grow lax and abusive of others on the supposition there will be no retribution. In the parable of the talents entrusted to servants for investment, He charges us with the responsibility of using to the full the graces and human talents we have received.

This responsibility for full use of our natural powers harmonizes with the fact that love of Christ makes us feel not less but more concern for the people and the affairs around us. "The joys and the hopes, the griefs and anxieties of the men of this age, especially those who are poor or in any way afflicted, these are the joys and the hopes, the grief and anxieties of the followers of Christ" (Pastoral Constitution on the Church in the Modern World).

That is why Jesus, in the final parable, the one on the Last Judgment, tells us that we must not merely wait for Him. We must love Him and find Him and serve Him in every need of the people around us.

When He finally comes visibly, His visible coming will cast light back upon His hidden comings. Only then will we discover that He came a long time ago into our lives, and stayed the while, as faith attests even now. We already possess God. We don't wait for that. We wait to see Him as He really is, and to become like that ourselves.

34

Who God Is

For millions God remains some Loch Ness monster reportedly sighted at odd intervals in history, but too elusively to be scientifically verified. Hundreds of millions of others believe that God has taken up "a local habitation and a name," and they love beyond measure the name God took. "The name Jesus was given to Him, the name which the angel had given Him before His conception."

Only a nation in touch with inner realities remembers the power and the radiance of a name. Who could be more insensitive or folly-ridden than the man who asks cynically: "What's in a name?"

The name *father* or *mother* or *child* contains an immense cargo of human wisdom gathered from the seven seas of life and sailed in from past ages to be unloaded upon the wharves of the present. The father who has not profited by the word he has inherited is no fit father, for without the wisdom of the ages he cannot know himself, and without self-knowledge he cannot be himself. And so with all the other words that carry the cargo of human experience across the centuries.

Ask the man who loves the name of his loved one. The name puts incense into the air and lights up the morning. It lets down a drawbridge into the heart of the beloved. When Mary Magdalene heard her name spoken as only One could speak it, it meant nothing less than resurrection from the dead of love itself.

The name "Jesus" had existed before that morning in Bethlehem when it was given to Mary's Son; but He, upon whom the name was conferred, conferred meaning upon the name. The meaning of the name was born that morning.

A breeze went out that morning and shook the name like leaves where it hung on the family tree of Jewdom. *Jesus,* or in Aramaic, *Yeshua,* was a common name at the time Christ was born. In former times, in an earlier form, it had belonged to Joshua, the successor of Moses. Joshua it was who at length led the weary people of God into the land of promise.

"Jesus" means "Yahweh is salvation." The name given Mary's Son by the angel before His conception is the name that belongs to Him alone, by identity with His substance, from His eternal birth in the Trinity. Like the name, Son, it is an inalienable name that tells who He is.

"You *must* name Him Jesus," the angel told Mary. The naming of God is a revelation that began when Moses, in trepidation at the overwhelming task appointed him, said to the mysterious Being who was sending him: "I am to go, then, to the sons of Israel and say to them, 'The God of your fathers has sent me to you.' But if they ask me what His name is, what am I to tell them?"

God answered: *"I Am who I Am.* This is what you must say to the sons of Israel: *'I Am has sent me to you.' "* And the *I Am* promised Moses: "I will be with you." By His very name, God has committed Himself to be, forever, *God-with-His-people;* that is, *God is salvation.*

What was told Moses was only being further explicated when God revealed by the angel that His Son's name in the flesh is Jesus. It was, too, only a further degree of presence when God's presence *became* flesh.

In the light of the meaning of this name, it is like watching men who have lost their senses and their minds to watch Christians who do not know God — who act as though God had not yet been revealed or were far away. To act this way is to deny the faith and to be worse than the pagans.

By giving us access to His personal name, God has established with us an intimacy heretofore unknown in religion. It is not something we can take or leave. To refuse this intimacy is to deny Christ.

It is an intimacy that must be lived by personal prayer and by devotion to the name. The Christian who fails to find time for prayer has failed to find time to be a Christian. The Christian who thinks devotion to the name is a mere pious practice has missed the boat. Devotion to the name of Jesus is the earnest commitment of human intelligence to one of the profoundest truths men have ever learned. *His name is a power He has given us over Himself. To know He is Savior is to know we are saved.*

Every Christian family shares the name of Jesus as its birthright. The Christian child does not receive a name until baptism, and the name he receives is a share in the name of Jesus. He is forever Christian, that is, *of Christ.* From then on it is the life and the name of Jesus that are his. One of the first words he has a right to have upon his fumbling tongue is Jesus' name. *Parents who don't put it there rob him of his birthright.*

From the "I Am" to "Jesus," God's self-revelation is a revelation of *God living with us.* The whole revelation of love in Christianity is also a revelation of God living with us. "God is love," St. John wrote, "and he who abides in love abides in God, and God in him."

That this is to be taken literally we can see by Jesus' promise at the Last Supper: "If anyone loves me he will keep My word, and the Father will love him, and we will come to him and make Our home with him."

This talk of love is talk of salvation. God is salvation, and salvation is love, and love is presence. Christ's love is salvation and presence. The *eros* of pagans could be a sad love that tortured with the absence of the loved one. *Christian charity is by definition love-with-presence.* We already possess God, and with possession of God goes joy, so charity is joyous love. God's salvation is joyous.

"Jesus," the good thief said on Calvary, "remember me when you come into your kingdom." And Jesus responded: "Indeed, I promise you, today you will be with Me in paradise."

The Christian has received the same answer. *Interiorly, he is dwelling where God is.* Hordes of Christians may deny this, but that is only a measure of their own unfaithfulness, or of the ignorance in which they have been bred by parents who have not jealously handed on to them "the name above every other name."

The name of Jesus is the constant reminder of where salvation must be found. Thank God we have put our hope in Him. "There is no salvation in anyone else, for there is no other name in the whole wide world given to men by which we are to be saved."

35

True Religion

Posted on the door of a friend's residence used to be the sign: "I've made up my mind. Don't confuse me with the facts!" I suppose the price of making a reflection like the following is the danger of a rude awakening — of discovering new responsibilities, of achieving a new maturity which awakens one to the obligations springing from friendship with God.

One man was thus rudely awakened, not by reflection but by event. For the future security of his family he had invested his savings in a piece of real estate in an affluent neighborhood. Some time later, as he drove up to his property once again, he saw peering out of the neighboring house a black face. His first reaction was the impulse to fire a shotgun at this threat to his family's security.

His second reaction was to be appalled at his first. He had always considered himself a devoted Catholic open to the whole teaching of Christ and the Church. "Is this what I really am?" he now asked himself. "What if I had died with a soul like this and appeared before Christ?"

To his eternal glory, this Catholic man was able to assimilate the staggering experience and grow by it. He had placed a profound act of true religion.

What is true religion? We are impelled to the question by contemporary social problems as they are illumined by the teaching of Jesus. "I assure you," Jesus warns us, "unless you have more religion than the scribes and Pharisees, you shall not enter the kingdom of heaven."

What is the root of true religion? The root is the discovery of God and the making of a personal acquaintanceship with God. "Enoch," we are told by the Book of Genesis, "walked with God." Enoch is the type of the religious man.

Enoch lived for 365 years, "then he vanished because God took him." This expresses the fulfillment of the religious man's hope for unending life with his God and Father.

The ancients, who lived closer than we to nature, could express this hope, and live the actualities of divine friendship, with greater ease than we. Their unscientific minds were open to superstition, but they were also intelligently sensitive to the realities lying beyond the ken of science.

To moderns, such prime human actions as eating and sexuality have, often, only the meaning of their physiological utility. For the primitive, writes Mircea Eliade, "they were sacraments, ceremonies by means of which he communicated with the forces which stood for life itself." The primitive recognized them as honored sharing in divine prerogatives.

The primitives were right in extending religion to the daily, palpable mystery of communion with the divine in the sphere of common diurnal activities. All genuine mystics continue this tradition. Its elements can be seen in the life of Dag Hammarskjold. Our modern insensitivity to these contacts has banished our religion to interior states.

And with the banishment has departed our sense of the immediacy of religion and its demands on us. When the demands are brought to our attention, we are shocked or outraged, because we never understood religion. We never understood that to be a friend of God is to be His helpmate in His project of creation.

"We offer Him our allegiance," says St. Augustine, "for 'allegiance' and 'religion' are, at root, the same thing." The pledge of allegiance to God and to His project is religion. By this pledge we open ourselves to the unknown cost of this mysterious friendship.

Who then is the religious man (we ask the question hoping to discover ourselves)? He is the man who walks through life with God. He is the man who dares to accept the risks of close friendship with God. He is the man who has hope in the future because the future is God's project. He is the eschatologically orientated man, for he waits to see God.

The religious man is the man who can still discover God in His world. The noble light of scientific understanding does not blind him to the nobler Light of the World.

The religious man is the man who belongs to man, for man is the prime godliness in nature. To love and serve God, the religious man must love and serve men, who are God's surrogates on earth, His very dear children.

The religious man is the man who puts God back into the places where He has been expelled by the history of sin. God comes to man as love, and the religious man fills the vacuum of love in the hearts of those he meets. God comes as food and drink and shelter, and the religious man puts Him into empty larders, and raises Him over the heads of the homeless. "Pure, unspoilt religion, in the eyes of God our Father" is caring for the orphan and the widow, and the needy everywhere.

The religious man understands why the Hebrew word for worship *('abad)* also means "work" and "service." The work and service should precede the worship to make us in some sense worthy of worshiping. Our Christian worship calls for preparatory holiness because it is the reenactment of the holiest of actions; and when entered into completely through Communion, it is an entrance into the holiest of events and the holiest of persons.

It calls, therefore, for the antecedent of lived religion. "Go first and seek a reconciliation with your brother," says Jesus; "then come and offer your gift."

36

Foundations of Religion

The atheist Sartre defines man as the desire to be God. History, it seems to me, rather displays man as the passion to be with God. Man clearly recognizes that his desire to play God is not himself but his infidelity. He discovers life to be the experience that compels him to raise his eyes high above the present time to the eschatological peaks beyond history where he will at last come to God.

The banquet to which Jesus calls men in the banquet parables is the banquet of life with God. But, as Jesus insists, we shall never attain to Him unless we are faithful to our passion for Him.

Faithfulness to the passion for God demands two activities: praying and obeying. By measuring them in our lives we can take inventory of our religion.

Neither praying nor obeying is easy. St. Bernard, that man of prayer, is said to have met a young man who claimed prayer was easy. The saint offered the man his donkey if he could recite an Our Father without a distraction — providing the youth agreed to enter the monastery if he failed. In the middle of the Our Father the youth blurted out: "Does the saddle go with the donkey?"

I consider praying one of the two foundations of religion because praying is our basic means of communication and communion with God, and no one neglects communing with the beloved. I grant all the obstacles to prayer, but personally agree with the observation of a priest-psychologist who said: *If we don't pray we don't love. Period.*

The parable of the king who gave a wedding banquet focuses on people whose mountain of worldly concerns is taller than their love for God. They wall Him out by their materialistic desires. They never reject God formally. And so they may even think they are religious and feel pious. They would be shocked if you told them they don't love God. *They just don't have time for Him.*

Obeying is the second foundation of genuine religion. It is easy enough to proclaim our love for God, but it is also easy to measure the truth of our proclamation. To know whether a tree is healthy, look to see if it bears its fruit in season. To know whether your love is healthy, look for its fruit, which is always in season. Love joins wills, and the fruit of the love of God is to do His will. "He who keeps My word," Jesus said, "he it is that loves Me."

King Saul disobeyed God when he took booty in war against God's will. The booty he took was cattle, which he planned to offer in sacrifice. "Does the Lord desire holocausts and victims," the prophet Samuel demanded to know, "and not rather that the voice of the Lord be obeyed? Because . . . *it is like the crime of idolatry to refuse to obey.*" Offering God what we want and not what He wants is adoration not of God but of self. Pretending to worship at His altar, we are worshiping at our own.

We are not aware of all of our disobediences in faith and action. When God warns us that the disobedient will never be with Him, some think they are doing Him a favor when they disbelieve Him in favor of their own interpretation of His love.

Or we may go to Church on Sunday, and on the way home drive like godless men. We may think it's enough to be good without being good for something. In the fourth chapter of his letter to the Ephesians, Paul tells us that the thief must not only stop stealing, he must also start working and start giving.

We may canonize our democratic sense of social equality as though it were unqualifiedly religious, when actually we so hedge it in that it is only the rude beginning of a Christly spirit. St. James wrote: "In your life as believers in our Lord Jesus Christ you must never treat people in different ways because of their outward appearance. Suppose a rich man wearing a gold ring and fine clothes comes in to your meeting, and a poor man in ragged clothes also comes in. If you show more respect to the well-dressed man . . . then you are guilty of creating distinctions among yourselves and making judgments based on evil motives."

What a furor arises when God's representatives among us command something difficult! How different from the response Jesus taught men to proffer divinely appointed authority: "The teachers of the Law and the Pharisees are the authorized interpreters of Moses' Law. So you must obey and follow everything they tell you to do; do not, however, imitate their actions, because they do not practice what they preach."

Catholics splinter into coteries and canonize the disruption. Of divisiveness and mutual accusation Jesus said: "Any town or family that divides itself into groups that fight each other will soon fall apart."

The contrast between the Scripture and our lives makes it clear where genuine renewal is needed. We need the change of heart Jesus demanded. We will not be able to make the sacrifice that praying and obeying demand, until we scale down our evaluation of mortal things so that we may be freer for eternal things.

We have to shift the ground of our lives to God and live for Him. Every heart was created that its possessor might live and enjoy God. Every heart but one. The heart of Jesus was made not to be used by Him but to be donated to us. It sacrificed its own inclinations to obey the law of the service of love. The response this should very evidently arouse in our own hearts is the clearest measure of what our religion should be.

37

Trying to Love God

"When you're tempted to question your wife's judgment," comes a sage's advice, "remember she had the good sense to marry you!" When we question God's way of doing things, we ought to remember that, after all, it *was* us He chose to create!

In creating us, God gave us the gift or "grace" of existence. The greatest of His graces is our rebirth in Christ. Basically, the word "grace" simply means "a favor." More technically, it means the divine life begun in us by baptism.

The theologian Peter Franson, S.J., draws from human interchanges of favors to explain God's gift of grace. In his book, *Divine Grace and Man,* he likens grace to the favor a princely young man conferred on a crude, coarse, ill-mannered and unloved girl by giving her his heart's love. She laughed at the ridiculousness of it, not believing in his love, not trusting his intentions.

He loved on in patience until her dormant personality began to germinate in the sun of his love. At length she laughed with joy and loved in return. His love had not only discovered her; it had created her.

What Franson did not add, however, is that with this girl's newfound love, new troubles were brewing. Love was beckoning her out of the turgid waters of her coarse environment to the rarefied atmosphere of a refined culture in which she would long have to struggle for breath.

Mankind is similarly tried in its love exchange with God, and for a similar reason. For love to run smooth, friends must be much alike and of equal social stature. Friendships, said Aristotle, can exist with limited inequality, of course. "But," he added, "when a great gulf is fixed, as between God and man, there can be no friendship."

The ardor of God's love has shattered Aristotle's dictum, not by ignoring the Law of Likeness, but by breaching from both sides the "great gulf" between God and man. God's Incarnation and our rebirth in baptism have made us friends.

The friendship is now possible, but that it is not easy is attested to by man's despairing struggle for fidelity, and by God's revelation. "Humble yourselves . . . ." Peter urges in his first letter, and tells us why. The struggle will be incessant: "Be earnest, be vigilant! Your opponent, the devil, is going about like a roaring lion, seeking someone to devour. Withstand him, strong in the faith . . . ." Scripture scholars think Peter was quoting the baptismal liturgy of the time. At our own baptism too, we were asked: "Do you renounce Satan? And all his works? And all his allurements?"

We do renounce them, but renunciation is not yet victory. Our love of God is strong and real, but so is our desire to "pluck the flower of the hour." Conflict ensues.

There is, however, not only conflict, but confusion. It is rarely easy to discriminate between the good and evil influences at work on us and in us. We are being lashed by a storm of facts and ideas "not according to the good spirit," said Pope Paul recently.

St. Ignatius Loyola wrote the helpful "Rules for Discriminating Between Good and Evil Influences." He says: "It is characteristic of the good spirit to give courage and strength, consolations, tears, inspirations and peace. This He does by making all easy, by removing all obstacles so that the soul goes forward in doing good."

The evil influences, whether from self or others, raise all sorts of false reasons and anxieties that discourage our friendship with God: "It's too demanding; it's downright impossible; it's really no more substantial than an LSD trip — which is much cheaper!"

Along with his Rules for Discrimination, St. Ignatius drew up the "Christian Strategy," which says that: the follower of Christ must subscribe to poverty (at least in the sense of detachment); he must graciously accept and even desire humiliations; and he must aspire to the genuine Christly humility these produce. Why? Because these are the Lord's own teaching.

His Strategy also warns us to guard ourselves against the evil influences. Their essence is to generate in us an insatiable thirst for wealth and honors (empty ones), which drive us on to pride — the precipice from which men fall to every evil, for pride makes men their own gods, and gods have no laws.

Even with this Strategy men fail. This means that not only must man constantly struggle, but God must tirelessly forgive. That is God's role in this love of ours, and Jesus tells us in the parable of the Good Shepherd that He brings back the stray, not complainingly, but on His bosom.

God is, in fact, more at ease with sinners than we sinners are. He scandalizes the straitlaced who whisper, "He eats with sinners," and the self-righteous who whimper, "God is dead," because He leaves men free to cause suffering — as *they* would not if they were God.

Suffice it to say that, as in every love affair, God and man hotly exchange charges off and on. "Evil from their youth," God says. "God is dead!" man retorts.

The bickering spews smoke and steam, but it can never extinguish the flame of jealous lovers. "For love," says the Song of Songs, "is as strong as death, jealousy as relentless as Sheol. The flash of it is a flash of fire, a flame of God Himself. Love no flame can quench, no torrents drown."

As long as there is sin there will be sadness; but as long as there is repentance there will be forgiveness — and as long as there is forgiveness there will be joy among the citizens of heaven and the denizens of earth.

Forgiveness and pity there will always be, for the Shepherd is much more concerned about finding the strays than the strays are about finding the Shepherd. If the lambs bleat, they will be found; if the prodigal sons return, they will be forgiven.

38

Man's Master

Drug addicts have lost the battle to be human — temporarily at least — and every one but the addicts recognizes that fact. There are, however, more subtle forms of addiction, and the slaves of them are even less aware they are slaves than are the drug addicts.

There are addicts to every form of pleasure and there are addicts to material possessions.

Whether you call him a voluptuary or a sybarite, the pleasure-seeker is the man who measures the success of his day and his life by the intensity of bodily gratification which he achieves. He thinks of life as a round of pleasures.

He may brag about the number of women he has seduced, or the number of tankards he has hoisted in a night, and how he was so "smashed" he can't remember how he got home. Thus he boasts about the accomplishment of reducing his noble human powers to less than the level of the beasts.

More sophisticated voluptuaries give a subtler but no more apologetic expression to their excesses. Their fornication, their adultery, their dishonesty in business are "indiscretions" which they expect any reasonable man to take for granted.

It is sad how such euphemisms hide the real nature of evil. St.

Paul tears away the sheep's clothing when he says flatly to the Galatians: "I warn you as I have warned you before: those who do such things will not inherit the kingdom of God!"

St. Paul was well aware how Christians set free by Christ could twist their newfound freedom into justification for every vice under euphemistic names such as our modern "relativistic ethics" and the terribly abused "freedom of conscience."

Paul left no one free to decide for himself whether fornication and adultery and other impurities were permissible. True to Christ, he condemned them thoroughly and definitively.

Pope Paul VI has followed his namesake in teaching clear norms of good and evil in methods of birth control. He too refuses to let euphemisms cover up the nature of evils which are destructive of man. Like St. Paul, he by no means denied any man's right to his own conscience, but also like Paul he by no means left formation of conscience to the inadequate resources of the individual.

We are supposed to be the masters of our bodies, not their slaves. The pleasure-seekers are their bodies' slaves. Their spirits have refused to wage the war against the flesh to tame it and subdue it to the spirit's higher aspirations.

The Christian must face up to the fact that the war between the flesh and the spirit was not pacified but intensified by Christ. He set us free to win the war, and saved us from hopeless surrender to our lusts.

Christ set the teaching Church between us and the self-deceits we employ to justify our desires. One of the most clearly other-worldly aspects of the Church is its strength in standing against the whole world to call evil evil and good good no matter how others pressure her to call good evil and evil good.

Pleasure-seeking is one form of a materialistic outlook on life. Jesus condemned every form of materialism. He warned us that we cannot serve two masters, for eventually they will give contradictory orders, and then we must choose one over the other. We cannot, then, be men of God and materialists, for materialism demands one way of life and God another.

If we do God's will we shall not destroy our human well-being but enhance it. Think of what a blessed place the world would be if there were no wars or murders or thefts or sexual immorality. The fact is that we cannot offend against Christ's law except by acts that debase us. We cannot serve Him except by acts that ennoble us.

It is true, however, that God does not will us to be well provided for at any price. Because of sin in the world there does inevitably come a time when we stand at a crossroads where the will of God and the opportunity for worldly benefits lead in contrary directions. It is then we reveal who our master is — Christ or the world.

"What weak faith you have!" Jesus says to those who worry. Men of strong faith have chosen Christ for their master, so they have little cause to worry. They do their best and leave the rest to God. They look on their efforts as cooperation with God, not as a substitute for God. Things can only go from good to better when they do His will. Since nothing is stronger than God, everything must work out to advantage for His friends.

39

Venus or Christ?

The blind man sat by the Jericho road, begging. What else could he do? Who is poorer than a man without light?

Yet this blind man was rich. His faith saw more than did the people around him with their eyes fixed on Christ. Those people, mute with the unbelief of the ages, tried to force their silence on the blind man. Lit by the light of his conscience, he shouldered his way up through the darkness and hollered: "Lord, that I may see!"

What is light? And what is sight?

Light is the rising-up of human consciousness out of the darkness which fills the stones and the plants, and circumscribes the lives of the animals.

Light is the intelligence and the understanding possessed by the only visible creatures made in the image and likeness of God.

Light is the radiance which emanates when good men work out their godlikeness in search of their rebirth as the "children of the light."

Dawn and light are symbols of deliverance from sin's darkness: "In the evening, a spell of tears; in the morning, shouts of joy," the Psalms say. Light is what comes when the Savior comes: "The people that walked in darkness have seen a great light!"

Light of light is the presence of God, who hovered over His creation from the beginning, even before He said: "Let there be light." He was a pillar of light during the desert sojourn, and He is the Light we await at our sojourn's end.

The True Light is the Suffering Servant who came into the world to execute the mandate given Him in Isaiah: "I have appointed You . . . light of nations, to open the eyes of the blind, to free captives from prison and those in darkness from the dungeon."

Jesus walked up to the blind man who had testified Jesus was the light, and gave sight. Jesus did this just after His own followers had displayed their blindness. They had heard Him foretell His own imminent humiliation, torture and death. They had heard Him describe what His love must do, "but they understood nothing of this."

To this day we followers of Christ are afflicted with that same blindness. Jesus commands love, and we think He is talking about Venus.

What is love? Love is God (but not God Incarnate; God Incarnate is wisdom). Love is self-giving but not self-surrender, for only the self-possessed can love. Love is the will in need of the mind, so as not to be lust. Love is tenderness and sweetness, tears and kisses and embraces, and union in the varying degrees foreordained by the wisdom of God.

The ancients had a different experience of love. They recorded it in the myth of Venus. Venus (or Aphrodite) was the goddess of love. Without her no joy or loveliness could be found. She was irresistible. She stole even the wits of the wise.

She was also jealous, petty, revengeful, inconstant and adulterous. When it came to fighting for anyone she loved, she was soft and weak and easily gave up.

Later poems portrayed her as treacherous and malicious and destructive of mankind. In them, her sacred sex orgies were recognized for what they were — adultery. Finally she was placed under male tutelage.

Some Christians want to dredge up Venus today in the name of Christ. They call love the only criterion of good or evil. They reinstate love as goddess.

If love is the only criterion of good and evil, how tell the difference between love and lust? "He who trusts his own prompt-ings," says the Book of Proverbs, "is a fool."

If love is the only criterion, why did Jesus give a different crite-rion: "He who has My commandments and keeps them, he it is that loves Me"?

Human love is blind without guidance. When Venus is in the ascendancy, Leviathan swallows the sun. To apotheosize any human value is to enter the darkness of idolatry.

Human love must be judged, like everything else human. "By their fruits you shall know them." The judge of love is wisdom. Without wisdom, love is a slave of sin. Venus was.

Love is not light. Love is the impulse to seek, to find, to hold. Christ is its light. Love is led by Christ.

The wisdom needed to lead love is divine, not human. That is why Christ is needed to be love's way and truth, and very life. Venus is without Christ, and she is the corruption of love. She dis-dains light, adores herself, and sins.

Christianity rests on the man Christ and the morals of Christ and the morals taught by Christ. Christ revealed the way not theo-retically but concretely and usefully. Christ did not extol Venus. He counselled the bronze girdle of celibacy for some; He demanded perpetual fidelity of the married; and He demanded purity of all.

He commanded a love which can be lived only by walking in His tracks. He Himself was guided, not by human intelligence alone, but by Scripture and revelation, for God alone possesses the wisdom man needs. "I do," said Jesus, "as the Father has com-manded Me."

Jesus is Logos Incarnate (Wisdom Incarnate), not Venus incar-nate. Love emanates from His wisdom. Wisdom is the principle of love. Love is not the principle of wisdom.

Venus is the betrayer of love. Venus' impulse is always "Now!" Wisdom responds that the time is not now, but in the *Kairos,* the time of the right and just conditions appointed by Creative Wisdom when He said, "Let there be light."

Venus' devotees say the only norm is love, but Paul, Christ's spokesman, gives many norms in the famous thirteenth chapter of his first letter to Corinth. What is impatient is never love; what is unkind is never love. Nor is what is uppity or snobbish or rude or selfish. What exposes others, judges others, treats others with cynicism or distrust is not to be fobbed off as love. What is iniquitous with adultery or any uncleanness is certainly not love. (Behold, Venus is a harlot fobbing herself off as love!)

Love is childlike innocence that has put away all childishness to go out to the loved one. Love is impetuous and ardent, but only — and this is the miracle — chastely, in the arms of wisdom.

Love in this world of sin is a suffering servant. The Son of Man "will be mocked, outraged and spat upon. . . ." Love must pass through death to come into inheritance of that eternal life which is its own offspring.

PART
FIVE

40

Freedom

Recently in Richmond I passed St. John's Church wherein Patrick Henry cried: "Give me liberty or give me death!" His cry was a prophecy which the whole world is taking up.

There is a freedom for which people are dying, and there is a freedom which leads to death. *Freedom is a heady elixir that brings life to those who master it and death to those who become enslaved to it.*

Freedom was always valued as the access route to fulfillment. Now even the ordinary man sees that it is much more. For freedom does not only lead to fulfillment, it is at the heart of fulfillment. Today freedom is consciously fought for and jealously guarded as that essential quality without which men and women are less than human.

Freedom can be given only by God, but it can be destroyed by men themselves in many ways. Ignorance snuffs out its flame. Passion and greed suffocate it. Prejudice is its grave marker.

Jesus Himself pointed out the source and the guardian of true liberty. It is His own resurrection that confirmed man's freedom. Jesus' resurrection is the escape route from the slavery of death and the access route to the freedom of life everlasting.

It is hard to realize the degree to which God's Son has freed the human spirit. He has come, says the Book of Hebrews, to "taste death for everyone," and to overcome death and *"deliver all those who through fear of death were subject to lifelong bondage."*

Prior to the resurrection, most men believed themselves in the clutch of a death that would never die. The world around them seemed to possess a more enduring being than they. Gripped by hopelessness, men slavishly grasped at the cosmic straw until death pulled them under.

Through Christ we have been freed from clutching at the cosmic straw, for in Him we possess more enduring being and life than it does. It is only since the time of Christ that men have been truly free to possess the world instead of falling into slavery to the world. It is with this understanding that St. Peter, in his first letter, gives us instruction on the use of our freedom in the secular city.

We use our freedom rightly, Peter explains, by submitting it to due authority, and by never surrendering it to the lures of earth. We must gain mastery over the cosmos by cultivating a free and sovereign attitude toward it, for we are greater than it and must never again become its bondsmen. We enjoy it not as our only good, but as our temporary home. We are, writes St. Peter, "strangers and wayfarers."

Two modern motion pictures depict in strikingly different ways the stance of the genuine Christian in the world. One is "Camelot," and the other "A Man for All Seasons."

Hollywood's treatment of Lancelot is an enjoyable spoof, but through it all the knight remains a remarkably prophetic figure who strikes sparks in every encounter with secular man. Anchored in God, his absolutes are beyond challenge, and his commitments have the ring of steel. Even his vanity does not obscure his earnestness.

St. Thomas More, "A Man for All Seasons," is no less firmly committed to the transcendental, but his absolutes are exceedingly unobtrusive in the ordinary course of events because they are appealingly fleshed out with all the urbanity secular man so esteems.

Then, too, St. Thomas More is a married man, while Lancelot symbolizes the vow of chastity which secular man considers a sword-thrust at the heart of his value system — mostly because he misunderstands it, but also because he understands only too well that, as an inflexible witness to man's eternal destiny, chastity stands guard over the sacredness and absolute inviolability of the source of human life, and therefore of human life itself.

Lancelot's absolutes are thrust rudely upon the world, not by his freely willing it, but by the inevitability of what he is. Lancelot has the metaphysical angularity and obtrusiveness of the prophet.

Sir Thomas More's absolutes are hidden and quiescent, uniquely his own — unless he is openly and inescapably challenged. Secular men find a Thomas More intriguing — even admirable — though when a conflict arises they demand capitulation to the world's standards.

St. Thomas More's mood is that of the cultured and cultivated Christian of every age. He is at home with God and with men. Lacking a crisis, his hand will never be called by secular men because they genuinely love that part of him which is identifiable with themselves. They admire too, the skillful fusion in him of manliness and godliness which simultaneously leaves him free for the world and yet lays claim at every moment to all he is.

The Thomas Mores are God's blessed gifts of reconciliation and peace to the world. They are gracious gifts of God, but they are not enough because they are not obvious enough. They demonstrate admirably how suitable the sons of God are for citizenship in any sane secular city, but they do not jar the complacent out of their sleep of death.

Many Thomas Mores are forgotten. St. Thomas More is remembered because a crisis arose which destroyed the affability of secular men and drove them to discover that in the end his transcendental commitments had the same ring of steel as a Lancelot's.

The Lancelots complement the Mores. Unurbanely they stride into the concourses of mankind and their fire and brightness awaken those who have fallen asleep spiritually. Irritated men try to thrust them aside but they do not budge. Angry men deal crushing blows but they do not break.

And if like Lancelot they should fall from their pedestals, even their ruins are noble, and in ruin they remain as powerful an influence as ever they were unsullied. It is not the good in men but the God in men that illumines the world.

41

Bad Faith

Picture a party of Czechs hostile to a certain Czech priest asking him: "Should we support the Russian occupation or not?" Realize that the question is posed not to get an answer but to lay a trap.

A "Yes" would condemn the priest in the eyes of loyal countrymen; a "No" would single him out for oppression by the occupation forces.

In the twenty-second chapter of Matthew, the priest is Christ, the hostile party is composed of Pharisees and Herodians, and the occupation forces in Palestine are the Romans. The aim of the hostile party is to get rid of Jesus by discrediting Him in the eyes of the people or disposing of Him through the force of Roman law.

The basic issue is not Church versus State but man versus God. God's troublesome message is once again threatening to upset (through Jesus) the prevailing order of things and the comfort of the established. The *establishment* is taking means to trap God's ambassador and reduce to absurdity God's message. When this fails, more "persuasive" steps will be taken.

The adversaries of Christ were acting in bad faith. They pretended — and perhaps had blinded themselves into believing — they were acting in behalf of religion.

The burning light of the Gospel makes us realize we are subject to the same bad faith. We have inherited centuries of entrenched resistance to Christ, and we have deepened the entrenchments by our own sins. We have hard spots against love and blind spots to truth.

Only gradually do the basic principles of Christ-life permeate the lives of His members. "Love one another as I have loved you," Christ commanded, yet how many centuries did it take Christians to realize this law of love dealt the deathblow to slavery? How long before we realize it dealt the deathblow to racism and every kind of snobbery?

Darken the picture further by realizing that we never win, once and for all, any battle against evil. Reverses are suffered in the advance of Christianity as in every war. The Christian conviction of the sacredness of life and the life source, which was so firmly entrenched in its victories a century ago, is reeling under the multiple attacks of abortion, euthanasia and contraception. Freedom for life has been distorted into freedom to take life, and God's laws are reduced to ridicule. They are not only unfashionable, they are "naive" and "obstructive to progress." It was just in those terms that Jesus was written off.

Let me cite some examples of bad faith which may infect us. We are all vulnerable to one or more of the following kinds of self-deceit: to believe God's word when it speaks of His mercy (heaven), and disbelieve it when it speaks of His justice (hell); to believe when He reveals the presence of the Good Spirit, and refuse belief when He tells of the evil spirit (Satan); to pretend that the forces of "law and order" do no evil, and to write off as rebels those who declaim against the social evils abetted by law and order; to act as though the other fellow or the other nation or the other religion were evil through and through, and as though we were good through and through.

Other examples are: *to pretend we admire the poor, virginal, dedicated life of Jesus while we condemn as misguided our own sons and daughters who feel called to re-live His life as religious; to admire the nonviolence of Jesus, while we write off as fools the men or women who counsel nonviolence as Jesus did, and who choose like Jesus to be beaten and murdered rather than defend themselves by killing their unjust aggressors.*

What then do we really think of Christ? Jesus counseled us to give aggressors more than they ask, but it took a non-Christian to disseminate His teaching. Mahatma Gandhi admittedly learned much of His nonviolence from the Sermon on the Mount. By his weak practice he helped to win independence for a mighty people without war — something unparalleled in the history of the world. Yet today Christians who advocate nonviolence are strangers in their own house.

Quiet examination into our own consciences may disclose after all that we too are in bad faith — that we are standing against Christ in some dark sector of our minds. We badly need the guidance of the Church of Christ and the Spirit of Christ to find out.

There are great storms in the Church today, and there are serious doubts, and there are real rebellions against the word of Christ. In the midst of it all we are reminded by Paul, in words of most serene confidence, that God "who has begun in you a noble work, by the same token will carry it through to completion right up to the day of Christ Jesus." God does not wilt before adversaries. God never changes His mind.

We will win with God, but only if we stand with Him. Paul would expect all of us to share with himself even imprisonment in "defense of the Gospel and its firm establishment." Surely no one is so hawkish as to claim it is dangerous to let fall all resistance to God. Only when we do abandon all defenses against God can we have every legitimate hope of sharing with Jesus the victory of immortality.

42

The Means to Discover Christ

Many lepers watched Christ from a distance, but St. Matthew tells us that of them all, only one said: "Lord, if you will to do so, you can make me clean!" Many fathers anxiously watched the sick members of their families, but only the centurion said: "Lord, my boy is at home in bed suffering terribly!"

What was different about these two people that enabled them to recognize Jesus and sparked their power to win miracles of healing from Him?

Sketchy though Matthew's account of the leper is, something of the reason for the leper's successful appeal is caught up in it. The account of the centurion is more at length, and the reason why he prevailed on Jesus is more evident.

By placing the curing of the leper after the Sermon on the Mount, Matthew implies that the leper's confidence in Jesus had been awakened by Jesus' teaching on human conduct. Jesus had defined right human conduct in such firm and certain terms that Matthew concludes his account with the words: "His teaching made a deep impression on the people because He taught them with authority, and not like their own scribes."

The leper recognized in Jesus that rare being, a man of authority. The leper had discovered that Jesus could address with power not only the world of man but the world of nature.

"Lord, if you will to do so, you can make me clean." The leper neither begged nor asked. With brilliant faith and a noble trust, he transferred his concern to Jesus. It was not cajolers and self-demeanors who reached Jesus, but people who believed in His authority, people who believed in it and believed He wanted to use it for their sake. The leper's implied request is very much like Mary's "They have no wine."

The centurion was even more clearly a man who would never sell his soul for a favor. Far from craven, his words and his request are freighted with dignity. Like the leper, he began by transferring his burden to Jesus: "Lord, my boy is at home in bed suffering terribly."

No man with a heart could be indifferent to those words. No good man with authority over sickness could stand inactive when another man had entrusted his need to him. The centurion was himself a good man with authority, and he understood this.

The centurion was at home with the power and feel of authority. It is clear from his description of its use that he loved authority. He wore authority as comfortably as an old pair of shoes. He knew its pleasures and its uses, but most of all he knew the good that it could do. He understood that authority was for the benefit of the subjects, not of the leader. His coming to Jesus for the healing of his son shows this.

No one can so readily recognize an expert as another expert. The centurion had made an absolutely certain and unerring identification of Jesus as a man of apocalyptic authority.

So certain was the centurion concerning the power of Jesus, and so conversant was he with the ways of authority, that he made the staggering request which left him a potential laughingstock of all the auditors: "Lord, I am not worthy to have you enter my house. Just give an order and my boy will get better."

Jesus had the power to respond. The great man stood vulnerable before Him. What could He do but one thing? "Go home. It shall be done in answer to your faith."

The centurion came to Christ through his common bond with Christ. We all must come to Christ through what we ourselves hold in common with Him, depending on our role. The father of a family recognized in Christ, the incarnate likeness of God the Father, a fatherly concern for all the children of men, and full authority to care for them.

The mother sees in Christ God's own maternal tenderness, wanting to serve and give. All lovers recognize in Jesus the love that commands absolute faith.

If we fail to be ourselves, we have no ground upon which to recognize Christ. The weak father does not recognize authority; the arrogant father does not understand authority that serves. The selfish mother does not understand or recognize love that gives.

By failing to be ourselves we undermine not only our own fate, but that of others. The man in authority who defaults in its use teaches the lie that there is no God. Authority used in a fatherly way reveals God's existence: "You would have no power . . . unless it were given you from above." Notice it is the atheistic Communists who teach the pipe dream that in an advanced society there will be no need for authority.

The current breakdown of authority results from the failure to use authority, particularly in the family. The father who knows little or nothing about the fatherhood of God eventually comes to think of himself as an assistant mother. The result is not only that his own role is atrophied and the children are maimed by being robbed of a father. The result is that God is eclipsed and atheism flourishes. This all comes about because God is revealed to us by integral humanity, male and female in their individual wholeness: "In the image and likeness of God He made him; male and female He made them."

If failure to use authority is a sin, so is failure to respect it. Whether it be a citizen toward his country, a member toward the Church, a wife toward her husband, a child toward his parents, or a religious toward his superiors, a person who refuses owed obedience is a denier of God. The willing obeyer is revealing the existence of God.

Authority helps to form character, and character produces hope in God. It is not only the spineless father who is a menace to the children. A mother who does not require obedience of her children spoils her labors for them.

Each cause has its effect. Religious faith is the belief that there is a Supreme Cause of all effects. He has authority over all causes. Individual causes have their effects only because He has authored them and endowed them.

Authority makes us turn to God out of reverence. The selfless authority of Christ awakened faith in the centurion. The centurion's reverence for authority wakens faith in us.

All authority selflessly used and rightly reverenced directs man's sight upward to Him whose creative voice once compelled us to leap the uncrossable void between non-being and being, until we stood at attention with the planets, the animals and the angels, and said with necessary obedience: "Here I am, Lord!"

43

The Transmission of Life

Resurrection life and food are mysteriously intertwined in the thought of man and the history of salvation, and the pairing demands our attention.

What are we hoping for when we hope for resurrection? We are hoping for a second gift of life to the body. We hope the more easily, once faith teaches us to realize that death is not a result of our bodies but of our sin.

The need for a second gift of life turns us to thinking about the source of life. As we know, the ultimate source is God, and the immediate source is those already possessing the kind of life to be transmitted: "Now Adam knew Eve his wife and she conceived and bore Cain. . . ."

God gave man provisional immortality: "You may freely eat of every tree of the garden, but of the tree of the knowledge of good and evil you shall not eat, for in the day that you eat of it you shall die." By sin man then forfeited immortality, thereby blocking God's plan for the transmission of ultimate life.

Adam's life was condemned in his flesh and Eve's. This condemnation is still in the process of execution. Their bodies died, but before death they passed on their flesh. We are inheritors of their living bodies. The flesh of Adam is still, literally, alive in us, but destined to die in us. The sentence is still to be executed.

Christ too inherited Adam's living flesh. The death sentence hung over it even in Him — and was paid. In Him God worked His justice yet took away its sting by mercy. The prophecy of what was to happen in Christ to reverse the tide of death and so of history was given in Psalm 16: "My heart exults, my very soul rejoices, my body too will rest securely, for you will not abandon my soul to Sheol, nor allow the one you love to see corruption."

Even in Jesus, Adam's flesh paid the threatened penalty of sin. In Jesus, however, God repealed the meaning of death. He made it something to rail at: "Death, where is your victory? Death, where is your sting?" God in His righteousness exacted His terrible justice, and in His passionate love He made it our glorious victory.

The first Adam is impotent to give us life uncondemned by sin. Christ, the last Adam, is not. Adam killed life everlasting by coupling it to sin. Christ pried death loose from sin by coupling death to innocence. In the Son of Man the risen flesh of Adam has emptied the tomb and come forth to be the principle of life everlasting.

The expected Messiah was prophetically identified as the "branch" who would spring up with new life from the withered vine of mankind. "Branching forth is His name," according to the Psalms.

This new Branch is the new Vine budding forth its own branches. "Just as all men died in Adam," wrote Paul, "so all men will be brought to life in Christ."

How does the last Adam communicate this life? The manner is beyond the compass of nature, but it has been foreshadowed in revelation: while Adam slept God "took one of his ribs and enclosed it in flesh. Yahweh God built the rib he had taken from the man into a woman, and brought her to the man." This text is understood by the Church as prefiguring her birth from the last Adam, from the blood and water poured out on the cross and poured into her through the sacraments.

The mystery of the transmission of the last Adam's life through sacrificial food is illumined for us by a venerable human tradition relating food to sacrifice and immortality. Primitives considered eating a holy act of communing with the divine force of life.

Semitic and other religions coupled eating with sacrifice. Sacrifice was gift-giving in which man offered himself to God under the symbol of the foods which sustained his life: cattle, grain and wine. He slew the animal, laid the gifts and poured the blood on the altar and on himself. He thus told God of his desire to share one blood and one table with Him, as children do with their father.

Man hoped that God would touch the gifts in acceptance, and by touching, transform them. Then, when he shared them with God at the table of the altar, the transformed gifts would transform him, making him a sharer in God's life, a son.

For ages priests spoke through ceremony and symbol. At length one Priest came and offered sacrifice without ceremony or symbol. The Priest was Christ. The victim was His body. Its transfer to God was by death. God's acceptance was the restoration of life. The communion of Christ the Priest in His transformed victim was His own resurrection.

Now it is our turn. For us, writes Durrwell in his book *The Resurrection,* the ascent to God is by way of "the journey through the immolated body of Christ."

Here we answer our question about how immortal life is transmitted. The new way of transmitting the immortal life which the first Adam can no longer give is by the nourishment of the Bread of Life in the mystery of the Eucharist.

For the last Adam, resurrection was a deeper integration of His bodily nature into His own Divinity. This gave His humanity not only life but life-giving powers: "The first man, Adam, as Scripture says," wrote Paul to the Corinthians, "became a living soul; but the last Adam became a life-giving Spirit."

We all change bread to flesh. Christ changes flesh to bread. The bread of His flesh is the way the last Adam transmits to our bodies the second gift of life we call resurrection. Not that the flesh in itself profits anything. Yet as it exists spiritualized in Christ it is the vehicle of the transmission of the Spirit of life. In Adam's Son, Christ, the flesh of Adam has regained its power to transmit immortality.

44

Religion Gives Life

It is strange how consistently we push to the back of our minds the fact that religion is a matter of life and death. Religion involves morality, so some reduce it to moralism; religion ennobles our affections, so some confine it to a search for warm feelings. *But the Good News that is the Gospel is the news of life.*

In the fifteenth chapter of his first letter to the Corinthians Paul summarizes the proclamation of the Good News ushered in by Jesus. His summation contains four points: first, Christ's death was for our sins; second, this was in fulfillment of prior revelation; third, Jesus rose from the dead on the third day; fourth, at the time of Paul's writing, many witnesses to Jesus' risen life were still alive.

A perusal of this particular Corinthian letter makes it clear that Paul's primary concern here is not Jesus' resurrection but our own. Certain Corinthians had denied the resurrection while still clinging to Christianity. Paul reduces their position to rubble: "If there is no resurrection of the dead, then Christ has not been raised; if Christ has not been raised, then our preaching is in vain and your faith is in vain."

We Christians ought to love life and health, but we ought to seek it in the right manner. Neither medicine nor science can give the People of God what the Supreme Being alone can bestow.

Today pseudoscience is heralding scientifically induced immortality as something just around the corner. Emanating from more reputable scientific quarters, however, is the observation that while science has removed obstacles to man's enjoyment of his full life-span, it has done nothing to lengthen the span itself. In fact, scientists are reporting the tentative discovery that our cells are programmed not only for life but for death. Even in cells there seems to be planned obsolescence.

We bid Godspeed to science in its valiant efforts to extend our lives, but we have committed our hope to One greater than all science. Our faith looks to Christ for immortality, and our lives must say what our faith does.

That is why the Christian Church is dedicated to life, and abhors everything that stifles it or terminates it. For if life is so good that we want it forever, and will have it forever, then surely the present stretch of life this side of death ought to be cherished as part of the continuity of eternity.

The Church does cherish it. She sees our current life and activity given direction and purpose by reason of its essential continuity with eternal life in Christ. She urges us to "put up a stubborn fight against any kind of slavery" that constricts life. She urges all men to deplore war, which so wantonly obliterates thousands and millions of lives in full flower.

She counsels us to teach the young peace and she praises those "who renounce the use of violence in the vindication of their rights . . . provided that this can be done without injury to the rights and duties of others or of the community itself."

She urges us to promulgate laws that "make humane provisions for the case of those who for reasons of conscience refuse to bear arms, provided, however, that they accept some other form of service to the human community."

She esteems the lives of all the children of God, and therefore she urges us on to the promotion of life in all countries by underwriting the economic expansion of underdeveloped nations with generosity that goes beyond justice. She remembers with approval the teaching of the Fathers of the Church: not to feed the hungry is to kill them.

Sickness, disorder and death are the enemies of man and therefore of God. What is God's enemy is doomed. The disorders of sin, sickness and death are doomed, and their demise is only a matter of time. "His enemies are scattered," proclaim the Psalms, "and those who hate Him flee before Him." Man too works incessantly to defeat these hostile forces, but man's work will never succeed except in conjunction with God's.

God has already established the strategy and the instrument of victory. His instrument is Christ working with us through the Sacrament of the Sacrifice. "O Lord," we pray in the postcommunion prayer for the twenty-first Sunday of the year (formerly the eleventh Sunday after Pentecost), "may we experience strength of mind and body from the sacrament we have received. Let it restore health to both that we may glory in Your heavenly healing."

In mysterious language the Apocalypse communicates a vision of God's final plan for us. It is a plan for life shared with its Author: "Then I saw a new heaven and a new earth; for the first heaven and the first earth have passed away . . . and I heard a great voice from the throne saying, 'Behold, the dwelling of God is with men. He will dwell with them, and they shall be His people, and God Himself will be with them; He will wipe away every tear from their eyes, and death shall be no more; neither shall there be mourning nor crying nor pain any more, for the former things have passed away.' "

45

God's Relevance to Man

The Gospels portray many incidents of people who came to Christ for earthly reasons without which they might not have come to Him at all. The ninth chapter of St. Matthew tells of a sick woman and a magistrate who came to Christ for reasons far less important but far more immediate than life everlasting.

The woman with the hemorrhage came only because the doctors had failed her. The magistrate came because he had a dead daughter whom all earthly help had failed. The mourners, engrossed in their pagan orgy of despair, did not come at all. They divorced themselves from the action of the girl's father, and ridiculed the prophet who came to them.

Death was death. *Finis.* The mourners would resort neither to God nor to His holy ones. Men do not come back from the grave.

These people had capitulated to time and mortality. They were prisoners of their own senses, and remiss in the use of their mind. They saw how seeds turned inert matter into life, and how the cells of their own body converted lifeless food into pulsing flesh. Seed and cell are tiny life-creating centers made by God and made evident to men, yet these people denied to God the very life-giving powers He had dispersed so munificently among the seeds and the cells of creation. Even before they insult our faith, they outrage our intelligence. For God, all things He chooses to have live, live.

Yet today's world is full of such people. They have "come of age." Inheritors of the millennia of man's efforts at universal conquest, they have their atomic power and their miracle drugs. With these they stave off death as long as possible without miracles. They have made their commitment to live for this world; and before that tyrant death they have hopelessly, cravenly run up the white flag of surrender. If they were the woman with the hemorrhage, they would put their whole trust in science; if they were the man with the dead daughter, they would drift dully with fate.

Statistics reveal that apartment-house dwellers are likely to be of this mentality. Ensconced in their synthetic environment, they display their divorce from God. They don't deny His existence. They just assert their indifference. They may even have an academic interest in religion. They play crossword puzzles and they read articles about religion, but only five to fifteen percent join God's People in public worship.

They say they don't fear God and they don't need Him. They don't fear Him because they have decided on their own authority that there is no life after death in which He will punish them. They don't need Him because they have decided there is no life after death which He will give them.

We are interested in learning from the mistakes of these people so that we may help both ourselves and them. Their basic fault seems to be not skepticism but self-centeredness. They don't look to see how lovable God is, but how useful He is. They find God relevant in their lives only to the extent they find Him useful in their lives.

They decide His place in their lives not as though He were a person but as though He were an article. Because they refuse to love, they remain blind. They end up without even the beginning of wisdom, which is to fear God. Much less do they have the fullness of wisdom, which is the love of God that casts out fear.

What is the correct way to assess the relevance of God in our lives? We must come to know God in love. Then we see at once that this Loved One, loved above all other loves, belongs everywhere in our lives. We soon come to know this is His sentiment too.

"I will release your captivity from all places," God promises us in Psalm 84. Whatever holds us captive is God's business. Nothing is so earthly it is outside the scope of His concern, or so distant it is beyond the reach of His power. "All things whatever you ask for in prayer," Jesus promised us, "believe that you shall receive and it shall be done to you."

Contrast this revelation of God with the sterile faith of some modern Christians who have lost their faith in prayer. Prayer is not mere petition. It is our ordinary manner of communicating with the God we love.

Prayer does not work like magic. Most of the time it does not work by miracles. It works in mystery. Prayer does not always bring us what we want. Yet if we persist it brings us what we need, and it converts us from wanting what we ought not. Prayer integrates our lives into a greater whole which includes all creation and all men and life everlasting through resurrection. Illumined by prayer, we withdraw our enmity to the cross of Christ because we stop living for this world only.

We lose our fear of death, recognizing it as the moment in God's plan when we will be "swallowed up in life." We await Christ, who will "give a new form to this lowly body of ours, making it into an image of His own glorified body."

Love is at the heart of life, and God is love, and found in all our loves. Religion is our love of God, and of all things in Him. From this vantage point, it is not the relevance of God which must be examined, but the relevance of all other things. All else must justify itself in terms of the one necessary relationship.

46

Transformation of Man

One day Jesus was transfigured on a mountain. Was the transfiguration simply a revelation of who the Son of Man is, or does it also reveal who we are? We find our answer in a careful study of the meaning of the transfiguration in the life of Jesus.

Jesus, the transfiguration reveals, is God's new emissary. He is an emissary more resplendent and more worthy of credence than the lawgiver Moses and the prophet of prophets Elijah.

Jesus came down from the mountain without tablets of the law in His hand because His own flesh was the tablet of the New Law. Jesus descended without any special prophetic words from God because He is the Word of God.

Peter, beside himself at what he witnessed, babbled about making three tabernacles for Jesus, Moses and Elijah to reside in. Peter and James and John were indeed to make three tablernacles, but not with hands.

The work that lay before them was a work no human power alone could execute. What the three Apostles were witnessing that day was a revelation of man's future. They were foreseeing their own destiny.

What is man, and what is his destiny? The questions are all-pervasive, and to answer them the Scriptures ask and answer many other questions.

What is the cosmos? Man is its crown and lord. What are the animals? Man is their self-transcendence. What is the kingdom of God? Man is its citizen. What is God? Man is His image and likeness. Who is Jesus? Man is the sharer in His destiny. In Christ, man transcends himself.

This Christ reveals, that man is the being most dependent on God, because his destiny is not self-fulfillment but self-transcendence. Man's part is to struggle unremittingly upward to the mountain of God. God's part is to lift man out of himself and into Himself.

This leaves man with the tense task of being wholly galvanized into cooperative action, and wholly passive in submission to God's own action in him.

That is why the meaning of the transfiguration for both Jesus and us is intelligible only within the context of its occurrence, which the three synoptics have preserved for us. They show that Jesus sandwiched in the event with forewarnings of His own suffering and death, and the sufferings of all His followers.

Who is man? Man is the being galvanized into action by the catalytic gap between his expectations and his existence. Man is the being who discovers the excruciating truth that his own powers even at their peak cannot close the gap. Man is the being who discovers through faith that he is destined for glory through suffering. "Don't tell anyone of the vision until the Son of Man is raised from the dead."

Peter was never to forget that moment of Christ's radiant glory, by which His transcendent identity was revealed. Not even the splendor of the resurrection could expunge it, for we have a reminiscence of it in the second letter of Peter: "We did not follow cleverly devised myths when we made known to you the power and coming of our Lord Jesus Christ, but we were eyewitnesses of His majesty. For when He received honor and glory from God the Father and the voice was borne to Him by the Majestic Glory, 'This is My beloved Son, with whom I am well pleased,' we heard this voice borne from heaven, for we were with Him on the mountain."

Sooner or later Peter understood that the transfiguration touched all of us, for in the same letter he tells us of our share in

Christ's transcendence: "His divine power has granted to us all things that pertain to life and godliness, through the knowledge of Him who called us to His own glory and excellence, by which He has granted to us His precious and very great promises, that through these you may escape from the corruption that is in the world because of passion, and become partakers of the divine nature."

Clearly, when we arrive at the Christian answer to the question, "What is man?" we come to understand why religion demands first place in man's life. Religion is man's one point of contact with God's world, which is the world of man's own self-transcendent fulfillment.

Within Christianity the sacramental mysteries are the specification of that point of contact. They join us to the Christ now eternally transfigured by the resurrection.

This reminds us that it is altogether wrong to think of our own transformation as something appointed for a future time. *Our transformation is going on now, in these mysteries, and in the business of our daily lives.*

Paul makes this ongoing transformation of ours quite clear in the third chapter of his letter to Corinth. To make God and Jesus the subjects of our thoughts, he indicates, is gradually to take on Christ's own likeness (just as fluorescent paint in the sun begins to glow with its brightness).

"And we all . . ." Paul writes, "beholding the glory of the Lord, are being *changed* into His likeness from one degree of glory to another." The word in the Greek, which is here translated *changed,* could also be translated *transfigured,* for it is the same Greek word Mark uses to tell of Jesus' own transfiguration.

Our transfiguration, like Christ's, can be seen, but in our conduct rather than in our bodies. That is a greater miracle than to have it seen in our bodies and not in our conduct.

The Greek word for Jesus' transfiguration is applied once again to our inner life by Paul in his letter to the Romans. "Do not be conformed to this world," he warns, "but be *transformed (transfigured)* by the renewal of your mind, that you may prove what is the will of God, what is good and acceptable and perfect."

Paul is again on the subject of our transformation in the fourth chapter of his letter to the Thessalonians. "Obviously," he says, "God has not called us to remain unclean, but to be *made holy* in Christ Jesus our Lord."

The manner of Christ's transfiguration reminds us how our own must take place. Luke tells us it was during prayer that Jesus was changed. Obviously, if Jesus could not control His destiny without the Father's help, we cannot. We cannot control even our own thoughts without God's help.

The origin of Jesus' radiance was not a successful fight to be supreme, but success in His efforts to be submissive. He battled Himself to the point of shedding His own blood to conquer Himself to the point of saying to the Father: "Not what I will, but what You will."

It is necessary that man abandon his plans for an unworkable closed-in secular self-fulfillment. Our works, joys and sufferings must go on, but with the meaning and the goal Christ has revealed. He leads us to cooperate in God's plan for our transcendent fulfillment. The way is outlined for us by the Word made flesh, and His flesh made radiant, and His body raised from the dead on Easter.

47

God's Devotion

One evening a bishop from India told me how the lepers come to his door begging. They hold out not hands, but stumps, to beg. They have no help, he said, but us. His companion told me about watching 500 women carrying baskets of coal on their heads, from a strip mine, up the hill to the processing machines. When they go back down they turn the gritty baskets over and put them on their heads as shields from the boiling sun. They have no soap to wash after work. They are paid twenty cents a day.

These things weigh heavy on my heart for many reasons. One of the reasons is that I learned a secret recently. I learned that because of the love Christ taught me for others I must now say: *Lord, what You do to others You do to me! What You let happen to them You let happen to me!*

Recently I described to a Sister the flamboyant placard I had seen last Easter Sunday proclaiming Augustine's words: "Every Christian should be all Alleluia!" The nun said: "Is that true, though?" She confessed her own depression. She finds it hard to go every morning into her eighth grade classroom. Her students are already imbued with the racial prejudices of their parents. When she teaches religion she meets the glazed eyes of children whose spiritual resonances have already been deadened, almost beyond hope.

The materialistic preoccupations of men are nothing new, as we see by the picture which Jesus paints in the parable of the banquet. It is a picture of people who do not love; they only desire. They are slaves of farms and cattle and one another. They know nothing of serving God, much less of loving Him.

"Christians who neglect to become the body of Christ," wrote St. Augustine, "know nothing about His body." A European sculptor, engaged to restore a statue of Christ broken during the war, conveyed a similar message. When he completed the statue, the outstretched arms were only stumps. "You," read the inscription on the base, "are the hands."

It is clear that God is not going to cure men's ills by miracles. The miracle He has given us is the victory of Christ, and the pouring out of the Spirit of His Love upon us ever since Pentecost. The next miracle requires our earnest cooperation: the miracle by which His Spirit in us makes us the hands of Christ transforming the world.

The parable of the banquet contrasts God's love, which invites us to the banquet of Trinitarian life, and our ugly, heartless lack of response which rouses God to both anger and further pity.

The gradual revelation of God's own love is the warp and woof of the history of salvation. Only after He had added man to His other creatures did God look over His creation and find that it was "very good."

As the centuries passed and man multiplied His abuses of God's creative love, God began to describe His love for His people as the love of a father who has carried His little son in His heart through the desert to the land He had promised.

In a still greater burst of love He described Himself as an ardent husband who clasped His bride to Himself and lavished on her every care — only to find her a loveless strumpet.

This did not put out the fire of God's love. He came Himself and loved us with one of our own hearts. His human heart has pounded with love for us, and thundered in fear of us, and broken with grief over us: "One of the soldiers opened His side with a lance and immediately there poured forth blood and water."

In an age when giving another your heart is a literal act, we should be able to grasp more readily the devotion to the Heart of Jesus. This devotion ushers us into the depths of the two greatest religious mysteries, the Incarnation and the Trinity.

The Heart of Jesus symbolizes the three loves with which Christ loves us. The first love is that sensible human affection which in deep love suffuses the whole body, so that it can be read in the eyes, seen in the countenance, and felt in the breast. The love of the heart is no metaphor. Medical evidence confirms human experience. The heart is so fully linked with the whole nervous system and emotional centers of man that it is the psychosomatic center of the sensible experience of human love.

In the resurrection religion of Osiris, which flourished in Egypt before Abraham was born, the heart was identified so completely with the mind and affections and life of man that it was considered to be almost the man himself. It had to be carefully preserved in death to assure the resurrection. It was the object which was weighed in the scales before Osiris to determine whether its possessor was worthy of resurrection.

The heart has a similar role in the Scriptures. It is the core of man. It is gross and fat with hardness and coldness, and stony with unbelief, or it is warm flesh pulsing with the divine currents of love and fidelity.

The second love symbolized by the Heart of Jesus is the love of the soul, of the mind and heart, of conviction and commitment. We offer it loyally and faithfully even when sensible love deserts us. It is the love which carried Jesus on, through acceptance and rejection, through life and death.

The third love symbolized is the divine Trinity's serene love for us, tender as a child's, yet beyond every other love as the sun's incandescence excels the feeble rays of the glowworm. It is the surging power of creation and redemption.

The parable of the banquet is an exhortation to smash our stony hearts into the pieces of repentance. Then God will give us a new heart, like Jesus' own. His is the heart in which God and man's love approach, identify and pulse as one.

48

Architect of the Future

Jesus once wept openly over a sinful city, and resolutely drove irreverent people out of the temple. And in his letter to the Corinthians, Paul lists our spiritual ancestors' historic infidelities and alerts us to the fact that "they have been written down as a warning to us."

The common denominator of the disorders which Paul recounted and which broke the heart of the strong Christ is the recurrent human refusal to meet God except on our terms. Man wants to dictate the terms or call off the friendship.

One of the most dangerous subversions of our fidelity to God is the one in which we band together in communitarian malfeasance — as though plurality established rectitude. "We have met the enemy," Pogo more sagely observed, "and he is us!"

The community is quick enough to condemn minority activity which is materially detrimental to the people as a whole. The community is, however, more loathe to condemn minority actions which give it some short-term advantage. If it lightens the tax load, immoral activity is not uncommonly ignored or even promoted.

Communities which adopt evil means to a good end are approving what God condemns, thus usurping God's role in the community. Such communities and the individuals who constitute them are a target of the warnings implicit in the lash of Jesus and the Corinthian letter of Paul.

Our problems in religious fidelity today very much arise from our social context. The atheists and false sheep among us promote their blindness to dim our sight. If there is to be light, we need the wisdom of God and His Church.

We also need the vision of foreigners who have not fallen into our blindness because they are not a part of our particular community. Someone looking in from outside can often point out the disordered values which have seeped into our souls and become so much a part of us we have come to count them as virtues. America needs her critics.

A South Viet minister admitted Vietnam needs us, but he lamented the devastating influence of our culture on his people. He cited particularly "rejection of authority, the equation of success with wealth, the insistence on ruthless efficiency."

Let us reinterpret this critique in terms of religion. It is saying that we are blind to God when He comes to us under the guise of right order. It is saying that the norm by which we judge good and evil is prosperity. It is saying we are more concerned with fashioning things than people.

These excesses are clearly distortions of what really are our virtues. Americans have taught the world much about freedom. Now Americans must be reminded in turn that freedom is a virtue only when it respects the freedom and the responsibility of others. And revelation reminds us that the greatest thing we can do with our freedom is submit it to the guidance of God. "The precepts of the Lord," says Psalm 18, "are right, rejoicing the heart — and His ordinances sweeter than syrup, or honey from the comb."

Slavery to hunger and disease is serious evil indeed, and American inroads against such slavery are highly praiseworthy. When, however, we begin to project the image of a people who value health of body over health of soul, we must reexamine the price we are paying for our affluence.

Efficiency is laudable, but it can also become a vice. The efficiency we achieve in material processes we try to transfer to social relationships. We see, by way of example, that society is increasingly ready to give its blessing to sexual immorality because its immediate social consequence can be warded off by medical or mechanical contraceptives. This is a process of substituting efficiency for morality. It is a process of dehumanization. It is also a process of abandoning God.

If we are not to fall into these traps we need to return constantly to God for His guidance and His forgiveness. We need to remember constantly that God's guidance is essential to us: "It is man's folly that spoils his fortunes," observes the Book of Proverbs, "yet it is against Yahweh that his heart rages."

Daily we need to remember and to live out our belief that it is not enough to build civilizations. We must build the right kind of civilizations. We have been given a blueprint by the Architect of Creation.

The plans call for the building of a civilization in which God Himself will feel at home when He comes. Our project is to build a civilization that is not a bandit's den but a cosmic house of prayer.

When Christ came to His city, He wept. What would He do if He came to ours? What would He think of the human temples desecrated by men's contempt for them because they are not of the "right" color? What would He think of the frail young temples falling to ruin from undernourishment in a land that does not have enough barns for its crops?

What would He think of the human temples burned to cinders or blown to bits because we have not yet loved enough to find a better way of solving our disagreements? What would He think of a country with so many billions for defense, whether we can afford it or not, and so little for the world's underdeveloped nations, because we think we can't afford it? To ward off possible danger to ourselves from other men we readily go into debt; to ward off the plague of hunger and destitution afflicting our own fellow citizens, we apportion inadequate funds and plead the need of balancing the budget.

Mankind is building a civilization which, sooner or later, Christ is destined to visit in person. We have the power to build it in such a way that on His return to the City of Man He will have no cause to weep again. Maybe, even, we can make Him laugh for joy. Man has seen God weep. What will it be like when we see Him laugh?

49

Suffering Preludes Theophany

Waves rocked the boat violently. The faces of the young girls showed terror. One addressed me worriedly: "I guess we are all going to heaven now!"

"Don't worry," I said with conviction, "getting to heaven isn't that easy!" The whole crew calmed down. We started to sing, and singing we put in to shore.

That reminiscence is a commentary on the frightening cosmic storm foretold by Jesus as the sign of the end-time. When the storm comes we are not to be afraid. We are to head singing for the shores of eternity: "When these things happen stand up straight and lift up your heads, for your redemption is near at hand" (Mt. 21:31).

We are pilgrims in a land exiled from the face of God. Pilgrims want Eden. Christ can restore Eden, so when He shall appear, we will at last know true joy.

Pilgrims on a journey expect hardships. They endure them in the hope of going home. It is in this spirit of expectation that Jesus told the Jews listening to Him to be glad when they saw their beloved Jerusalem leveled to the ground. When we see everything that resists God being swept away, our joy ought to outweigh our sorrow, for it can mean only one thing: *God is on the way.*

Suffering preludes theophany. It is a purgative event preparing for the visit of God, who cannot enter pigpens of human corruption. Whether it is a matter of God coming to us individually (as at death) or collectively (as at the Parousia), there is first the cleansing suffering, and then the Arrival.

Christ asks us to suffer with joy, because all suffering can be purifying. If all our joy disappears when suffering comes, and if our faith is shaken, it is probably because we have no conviction of the true horror of sin, and no knowledge of the invasions of suffering God permits to destroy sin.

The mystery of suffering is not solved by revelation, but it is illumined. Sin is punished by its own effects. *People have come to dissociate sin and suffering, but this is a lie.* Suffering does come from sin (though not all suffering), but the sufferer is not always the one who sinned, and the sinner does not always suffer in this life.

One need be no religious genius to see the suffering that follows in the wake of adultery, lawlessness, drunkenness and dope addiction. Even sins against reason such as living beyond one's means bring untold sufferings.

People today who foolishly expose themselves to dangerous radiation are accumulating a store of defective genes that will plague generations yet unborn. So too sins against God done in the past visit their moral and physical evils upon us the living. Our own selfishness and irreligion are being stored like an evil bequest for generations to come.

God permits suffering, not only to purify us, but to prevent and inhibit further sinning. The obstinacy of sinners in their sins is almost beyond belief. What suffering can anyone name as a sure remedy for turning even one sinner from his immorality? Not war, or disease, or death in the family will certainly succeed.

The Book of Revelations tells of the almost merciless punishments God visits upon men "less something worse befall you." Yet, after one terrible punishment, we read that "the rest of mankind, all those who had not been killed by these plagues, did not turn away from what they themselves had made. . . . Nor did those men give up their murders, their magic, their immorality, or their stealing."

God does not want to let us suffer, but He will even send us suffering rather than have to come and find us unprepared. "You do not have what you want," St. James wrote, "because you do not ask God for it. And when you ask you do not receive it, because your motives are bad. You ask for things to use for your own pleasures. Unfaithful people! Don't you know that to be the world's friend means to be God's enemy?"

Whatever stands against God will be converted or will be swept away in the course of history. That is the preparation for Christ's coming. This era of the ongoing establishment of the Church-Kingdom is the era of the long Advent. It is an era of suffering that can be joyous. Dying to the old, we are being born into the new creation. Suffering is the growing pains of life everlasting.

Luke reports that, after talking about the final times, Jesus Himself warned that we must "stay awake, praying at all times," and avoiding all excesses, lest "that day will be sprung on you suddenly, like a trap."

Luke adds a few words describing Jesus' own last days on earth. "In the daytime He would be in the temple teaching, but would spend the night on the hill called the Mount of Olives."

Jesus ends the frightening account of the final times by comparing those terrible signs preceding His coming with the swelling buds that usher in the spring. What look like terror and death are only the last fitful storms of the winter of sin being displaced by the springtime of everlasting love.

50

We Have a King

The Angel Gabriel revealed and the Virgin Mary accepted. Then the royal wedding of Godhood with manhood proceeded. The oil of Divinity was poured into the water of humanity, and what cannot be mixed yet became one.

The Son, begotten from eternity by the Father, was given to Mary to be clothed in her nature and become one of us. With His human nature He took the human name, Jesus, but His human name disclosed His divine nature. "Jesus" means "Savior," and only God can save. The Scripture curses the man who puts his trust in a man. Jesus' human name discloses His Godhood.

Jesus is the man born to be our King. His royalty derives from His divine origin which antedates His conception into this universe. "In the beginning was the Word, and the Word was with God, and the Word was God." He existed not only prior to His own humanity, but prior to all created things. In fact, He created all things.

"Crown Him With Many Crowns," for Christ the King has yet other claims to our loyalty besides His anointing with Divinity. He gave His mortal life for us in a royal sacrifice which terminated in His birth into immortality by resurrection, thus establishing Him as the root of the vine of life everlasting. "He is the beginning, the

firstborn of the dead, that He may hold first place in everything."
He is the Life of the citizens of His Kingdom.

This King is the mystery hidden from eternity which is in the
process of revelation. The mystery can be revealed only by the ongoing establishment of His kingly reign, for He cannot be known
without His people. He and His people are one.

His Person is the greatest mystery ever to cast effulgence upon
this earth. His humanity is the arrowhead of the penetration of
Divinity into the universe.

Whenever we look at Him we see both perfect humanity and
perfect transcendence of everything human. His body lived like
ours, and died as ours will, yet it is the sacrament of all future life,
and it is among us now.

His heart pulsed with every worthwhile human emotion, yet it
poured into the world such a river of transcendental hopes and
loves that its so-perfect humanity lights up in an unearthly way the
world beyond man to which men are invited.

He lived as a child in Nazareth and there, choosing the career
of His foster-father, He became a carpenter. His work was human
work, yet everything He did shames and condemns the religious
secularist for it all had upon it the transcendental mark of man's
calling: "Did you not know I must be busy with My Father's affairs?"

Though He was born to be King, His kingly rule has upon it
the mark of the servant, for to Him, to rule is to serve: "The Son of
Man came upon earth not to be served but to serve." The mystery
of a King-servant is illumined by remembering that He addresses all
the members of His Kingdom as "My brothers and sisters."

The servant nature of His rule does not diminish but rather in-
tensifies our obligation to obey. Rebellion is not only marble-heart-
edness and fiendish ingratitude, it is self-destruction. It puts us
beyond the perimeter of His redemptive work.

Christ's kingly reign is not "of this world." It has no taint of violence or sin, which infects every earthly kingdom. It refuses to use
force: "If My kingdom were of this world, My subjects would be
fighting to save Me," Jesus said to Pilate.

Jesus' kingly reign is, nevertheless, very much in this world.
"He is before all things, and in Him all things hold together." Men

in this world are torn apart by only one thing — sin — and they are joined by only one thing, the peace of His blood and His reign.

His reign reaches to all things through man. His gentle rule reaches men from within, through their consciences. His light also illumines men from without, through the handing on of revelation, through the living Church, and through legitimate civil rule.

Not by the use of force, but by being Truth refulgent, beckoning and commanding as only Truth can, Jesus is the Ruler of the rulers of the earth.

He who controls the mind and heart of man controls the destiny of the universe. Christ the King has the right to the reign of truth and love over our hearts. The day we obey Him and not before, we will rule the cosmos. There is no other way.

Every year on the Feast of Christ the King, pastors have a papal mandate to consecrate their parishes and the whole world to the Sacred Heart of our King present in the Blessed Sacrament. It would please the King if we added our own personal consecration in words such as these:

Jesus Christ my King, I consecrate to you my life, my labors and my possessions. I will work like You to make Your justice, truth and brotherly love prevail in the world I inhabit. Should poverty and oppression result for me as for You, I am ready to endure them to make Your kingdom come.

51

Cosmic Continuity

My father was very wise in the ways of Easter. For Easter he used to give us live Easter bunnies. We experienced the Paschal season as the time of warm, friendly new life.

Easter is obviously the feast of life, but the mystery hidden in the new life of Jesus is no more obvious than Jesus Himself was on the morning of the resurrection.

The discovery of Jesus' rising was quite complicated. It did not begin with ecstatic women having a vision. It began with very distressed women saddened to discover the empty tomb.

When the followers of Jesus did see Jesus that day, they had difficulty recognizing Him and accepting the mind-shattering fact of His resurrection. The Gospel accounts are earmarked with the shock and disbelief as well as the joy of that day.

The Vigil Mass of Easter sheds such light on this difficulty of recognition that it makes us realize that the lack of such difficulty would be far harder to explain.

The Vigil service begins with the striking of a spark from the rock. The rock is God, and the new spark is the risen life of Christ. The reading that follows recalls the origin of life in the creation of Adam and Eve. The second reading is a prefigurement of the freeing of the chosen people from the slavery of sin and death. The third reading prefigures the future washing-away of sin and immersion in Christ's life through baptism.

This perspective is necessary to understand both the resurrection and the difficulty of recognizing the risen Jesus. The readings put in order the steps of God's creative action. God's creativity involves an ongoing process in which new life is not always simply a repetition of what went before, but an addition to what went before.

Jesus' new life is not just something fresh but something unique. His resurrection is not a restoration but a transformation, not a return to mortality but a bestowal of immortality. Jesus did not return to the status which preceded His death. He advanced to the definitive state of humanity which God destined from eternity and created for mankind on that first Easter.

Through Isaiah God had foretold this newness He would bring about: "Behold, I create a new heaven and a new earth." Jesus is the new earth who is also the new heaven. God climaxed His work of creation by re-creating the last Adam on the first Easter.

St. Paul was describing this new kind of newness when he told the Corinthians that the risen body is changed as profoundly as the planted kernel which rises as a stalk of wheat. The body that dies is perishable, dishonored, weak, material; it is raised imperishable, glorious, powerful, sharing divinity.

If a whole body of water can become intangible through evaporation, it should not seem too strange that the body of Jesus transformed through resurrection should not be accessible to the senses in the same way as His mortal body. The followers of the risen Jesus needed faith to reach to Him in His new life.

Yet they did reach to Him with His help. They saw Him and watched Him eat. They listened to Him talk. They received the invitation (which Mary Magdalene did not wait for) to feel Him and see that He was no ghost. Thomas was invited to examine His scars and know that it was truly He, Jesus.

The core of the Christian Good News from the beginning was that Jesus rose and His followers saw Him risen. The Apostles thought of their apostleship as a work of witness. They were eyewitnesses to the resurrected Jesus. Their criterion for choosing a man to replace Judas was that he be one who could give eyewitness with them. St. Paul indicates there were some 500 eyewitnesses to choose from.

The Apostles risked their lives to give this witness. "You killed Him," Peter said boldly to his fellow Jews, "but God raised Him to life. . . ." Peter's enraged listeners wanted to kill him on at least one occasion in the very beginning. In the end he gave his life in witness to the new life of Christ which he planned to share.

The witness which Peter and the Scriptures and the whole Church give is not to Christ's resurrection alone, but to our own. Our own resurrection is dependent on the resurrection of the very flesh which Jesus received from Mary.

Peter insistently points out that the Psalms had foretold the preservation of the flesh of the Anointed One: "My body too will rest in hope that you will not abandon my soul to Hades nor allow Your Holy One to experience corruption."

At issue in the preservation of the flesh of Christ is the continuity of God's creation and therefore His total triumph over sin. Life came in the beginning from God, in the interim from Adam, and in the final times from the Last Adam. The Last Adam is in continuity with the first in His flesh, but in continuity with the divine Father alone in His life.

This makes the body-person of the risen Jesus the sole source of the spread of resurrection life: "The first man, Adam, as Scripture says, became a living soul; but the last Adam has become a life-giving spirit. . . . And we, who have been modeled on the earthly man will be modeled on the heavenly man" (I Cor. 15:45-49).

The body of Jesus is the sacrament of transference, but the source of the new life He transmits is His Holy Spirit. That is why Jesus could say, "Unless you eat of the flesh of the Son of Man and drink His blood, you shall not have life in you," and yet add: "It is the spirit that gives life, the flesh profits nothing."

Our risen life is made more tangible by this scriptural emphasis on the bodily continuity in the transmission of life. *The mode of transmission changes, and the kind of life transmitted changes, but there is continuity from the primeval man, the first Adam, through intermediaries, to the Last Adam, the final model of man, the eschatological Man, Jesus Christ.*

Toward the end of his life Paul began to speak of our resurrection as an accomplished fact. He wrote the Ephesians that "God loved us with so much love that He was generous with His mercy; when we were dead through our sins, He brought us to life with Christ. . . . and raised us up with Him, and gave us a place with Him in heaven, in Christ Jesus."

This is in accord with the teaching of Jesus that faith, baptism, and especially the Eucharist, have already implanted Him, the seed of immortality, into our persons. "He that eats My flesh and drinks My blood," Jesus taught, *"has* everlasting life, and I will raise him up on the last day."

Like a child's soul, which he possesses at infancy though it can only gradually transform him into a full-grown man, the being of Christ is already joined to us and is gradually transforming us into the likeness of His own resurrection, first in soul, and later in body. That is why Paul, who is always practical, urges us to live by the new life we already possess.

"Since you have been raised together with Christ," we find Paul saying in his letter to the Colossians, "seek the things above, where Christ is seated at the right hand of God." Paul adds a promise: "When Christ, who is our life, appears, then you too will appear with Him in glory."

The Church and its members are in possession of the resurrection because they possess the body of Christ. They justly and rightly give thanks to the Father because every Easter and even every day they both celebrate and share the resurrection of Jesus by eating the feast of the Paschal Lamb.

OTHER BOOKS FROM OUR SUNDAY VISITOR

THE TRIAL OF CHRIST
by Father Ralph Gorman, C.P., 200 pages, paper $2.95.
This reappraisal of Christ's trial and Crucifixion suggests a more reasonable sequence of events in the last hours of Christ's life. Father Gorman takes a critical look at the chronological possibilities and probabilities of Christ's arrest, conviction and execution.

CATHOLIC ALMANAC
edited by Father Felician A. Foy, O.F.M., 704 pages, cloth $7.95, paper $3.95.
This book is the most complete single-volume of facts and information concerning the Catholic Church. It contains the Liturgical Calendar, lists of Church officials and Catholic organizations, biographies, a glossary, statistics, many statements and reports on contemporary developments, and much more. It is revised and updated annually.

WHAT DIFFERENCE DOES JESUS MAKE?
by Frank J. Sheed, 242 pages, paper $2.95.
In this age of *Superstar* and "Jesus Rock," young, zealous Christians are knocking on the door of the establishment with this haunting question. The author answers not with stifled jargon or meaningless rhetoric but with soul-searching dialogue. Using Christ's own words and applying Scripture to today makes the difference.

If your bookseller does not have these titles, you may order them by sending listed price (we pay postage and handling) to the Book Department at the address below. Enclose check or money order — do not send cash.

Write for free book list

Our Sunday Visitor, Inc. / Noll Plaza / Huntington, Ind. 46750